DEC

DISCOVER CANADA

Manitoba

By Ken Emmond

Consultants

Desmond Morton, FRSC, Professor of History, University of Toronto

John Einarson, Teacher of History, St. John's-Ravenscourt, Winnipeg

 Grolier Limited
TORONTO

Winnipeg skyline.
Overleaf: Sunset on the Hayes River.

Canadian Cataloguing in Publication Data

Emmond, Kenneth D. (Kenneth Donald), 1941-
  Manitoba

(Discover Canada)
Rev. ed.
Includes index.
ISBN 0-7172-3139-9

1. Manitoba — Juvenile literature. I. Title.
II. Series: Discover Canada (Toronto, Ont.).

FC3361.2.E55 1996   j971.27   C96-931033-1
F1062.4.E55 1996

Front cover: Rolling farmland near Bruxelles
Back cover: Assiniboine Park, Winnipeg

Printed and bound in Canada.
Published simultaneously in the United States.
  3 4 5 6 7 8 9 10   DWF   99 98 97 96

Fishing at Tulibee Falls.

Table of Contents

CHAPTER 1
Canada's Keystone Province

Manitoba is known as the Keystone Province and a glance at a map makes it easy to see why: like the keystone in an arch, the province lies right in the middle of Canada. And that's not all. It is also right in the middle of North America, halfway between the Arctic Ocean and the Gulf of Mexico as well as halfway between the Atlantic and Pacific oceans. The capital city of Winnipeg is about as far as you can get from any ocean.

Since long before history was written, people have come to mid-continent to trade at the Forks, where the Red River meets the Assiniboine in the heart of present-day Winnipeg. Natives from the eastern and northern forests and the western and southern plains exchanged goods there thousands of years ago.

More recently, in the late 1800s, European settlers began pouring into the Canadian West. Most of them had to pass through southern Manitoba, and many decided it would be a good place to start a new life. Winnipeg turned into a boom town as demand sprang up for a host of services, and soon the province had earned its reputation as one of the most ethnically diverse communities in North America.

Manitoba's days of boom towns and rapid expansion are over, but the province still has a solid record of slow, steady growth. And people still come, look around, and decide that there are lots of ways to prosper and enjoy life in the Keystone Province.

The Forks. The historic junction of the Red and Assiniboine rivers has recently been reborn as the meeting place it was for thousands of years.

CHAPTER 2
The Land

Many people think of Manitoba as an agricultural province, and it is true that farming has played a key role for 150 years. But almost all of the province's farmland lies in the south and southwest part of the province, inside a triangle formed by the Saskatchewan and U.S. borders and a line drawn from the southeast corner to Flin Flon. This area takes up only about one-fifth of the province's 650 000 square kilometres (251 000 square miles).

The northern three-fifths of the province is inside the Canadian Shield, where the landscape is dotted with lakes and bogs, and where the most important resources are minerals, forests, fish and energy. The remaining one-fifth is located in the extreme northeast, where the forests give way to treeless tundra. Manitoba is thus the least "prairie" of Western Canada's three Prairie Provinces.

The Legacy of the Ages

Two great events, an unimaginable billion or more years apart, shaped Manitoba's geography.

The first took place more than 1.5 billion years ago and created the Precambrian Shield. The second carved the landscape that was here when the first people arrived a few thousand years ago.

Anyone familiar with the province will find it difficult to believe, but Manitoba has gone through two periods of volcanic activity and mountain-building. It's hard to picture a mountainous Manitoba with towering peaks dominating the landscape. It is also difficult to

Overleaf: **Sunflower field near Altona. Almost 90 percent of Canada's sunflower crop is grown in Manitoba.**

Manitoba's varied landscapes. Inset into the aerial view of southern Manitoba farmland are, left to right: coniferous forest and cliffs over-looking the Poplar River, east of Lake Winnipeg; the Hudson Bay shoreline on July 1; Precambrian rock on the tundra.

grasp that by the start of the Cambrian Era, about 570 million years ago, the mountains had eroded away almost to sea level!

The Precambrian rock formations, dotted with lakes and punctu-ated with swift-flowing rivers, form some of Manitoba's most spectacular scenery. They also hold its storehouse of mineral wealth — the nickel, copper, zinc, lead, gold, silver and tantalum that come from its mines.

Slowly, over eons of time, the bedrock was covered by varying thicknesses of dust, silt, rocks and other debris. This material is called sediment. Over millions of years, a layer of sediment piled up in different parts of Manitoba — a layer so deep it would not have been measured in metres or feet but in kilometres or miles.

Some of these sediments have commercial value. For example, the sedimentary rocks formed more than 200 million years ago in southwestern Manitoba contain petroleum. Limestone at Garson and Stonewall, just outside of Winnipeg, is used in construction. So is the gypsum from deposits south and west of Lake Manitoba. It was formed from countless billions of corals and other living things within the last 100 million years.

The second key geological event took place almost yesterday in terms of the Earth's history. It was the advance and retreat of the last Ice Age glacier across Manitoba. Several times in the past two million years, huge glaciers advanced over much of the world. They stretched much farther south than today's polar ice. In North America, the most recent advance of the ice sheets started about 75 000 years ago. For nearly 60 000 years, Manitoba was buried under an immeasurable thickness of ice.

A global warming trend began about 16 000 years ago. After almost 5000 years, the southern tip of the glacier covering Manitoba melted, and land began to re-emerge. But the melting ice had nowhere to flow, and so it formed an immense lake — Lake Agassiz. At its largest, Lake Agassiz spanned 350 000 square kilometres (135 000 square miles) — more than all of the Great Lakes combined — and covered most of Manitoba as well as parts of Ontario and of present-day Saskatchewan, North Dakota and Minnesota.

Land erosion and melting patterns constantly changed the size, shape and depth of the lake. With its northernmost area still under the glacier, Lake Agassiz was always as cold as the ice that buried its northern shores. As great chunks of ice broke off into the lake, it must have looked like a polar ocean.

Huge, fast-flowing rivers, as wide as the Mississippi River at its widest, poured glacial meltwater into Lake Agassiz. The valley

12

Lake Agassiz, formed about 11 500 years ago, was the biggest glacial lake in North America.

floor carved by these icy rivers are part of today's landscape. The broad valleys of the Assiniboine River in western Manitoba and the Pembina River in the south are examples of small modern rivers dwarfed by the beds of the glacial rivers of the past.

The Ice Age is still changing the land in northern Manitoba. The huge ice sheet caused the land to sink, but the land slowly began to rebound as the ice melted. In the south, the land has finished rebounding, but in the north, the glacier's final retreat is so recent that the earth is still rising, on the average by about a centimetre (0.4 inch) every year.

Elsewhere, the incredible pressures of ice sheets, the grinding of rocks, erosion, and past movements of debris from one place to another, dictate the shape and texture of Manitoba's surface. Today, the province slopes gradually downward from the southwest to northeast, like a saucer tipping gently into Hudson Bay.

Right: One of Manitoba's surprises — a small, but very real bit of desert. Called Spirit Sands, it covers about 25 km² (10 sq. mi.) in Spruce Wood Provincial Park. *Far right:* Pisew Falls is one of Manitoba's loveliest waterfalls and the highest one that can be reached by road.

By about 5000 B.C., most of Lake Agassiz had run off. The silt and clay that remained now provide the rich soils of southern Manitoba. A unique landscape feature in Manitoba is the Carberry Desert, located where the glacial Assiniboine River flowed into Lake Agassiz. Manitoba's "mountains" were formed from debris remaining when the receding glacier stopped for a few centuries. The highest point, Baldy Mountain in Duck Mountain Provincial Park, is 831 metres (2726 feet) above sea level. The inland cliff, located on the eastern edge of these mountains is called the Manitoba Escarpment — which also formed the western edge of glacial Lake Agassiz. Numerous "glacial beaches" can be found along the escarpment.

Lakes and Rivers

Lake Winnipeg, Lake Manitoba and Lake Winnipegosis are the three largest survivors from the Ice Age. The province has almost 100 000 other lakes and countless marshes left after Lake Agassiz drained off into Hudson Bay.

All of Manitoba's rivers and lakes eventually drain into Hudson Bay. The Nelson, Churchill and Hayes rivers flow directly into it. The Winnipeg, Saskatchewan and Red rivers and their tributaries flow into Lake Winnipeg, which in turn drains into the bay through the Nelson.

In all, water covers over 15 percent of the province's total area.

Wildlife and Vegetation

As the ice sheets receded, a variety of animals roamed over the forest and tundra regions that emerged. Among the animals of the time were sabre-toothed cats, the giant bison, the giant beaver, lions, horses and several kinds of now-extinct members of the elephant family.

Vegetation changed as the climate became warmer. At first, forests dominated by spruce trees took over from the tundra. Then, as the warming continued and the climate became drier, the southernmost forests began to give way to grasslands, or prairies.

Today, Manitoba has more than 350 species of birds, mammals, amphibians and reptiles.

Barren ground caribou migrate south into Manitoba in winter, and polar bears breed on the shores of Hudson Bay in the summer. Beluga whales and four species of seal are also found along the bay coastline. Shield country is home to black bears, wolves, deer, elk, moose and many kinds of small fur-bearing animals such as beaver and muskrat. Smaller predators like the lynx and bobcat are common in southern agricultural areas, where their favourite prey — rabbits and rodents — are plentiful. Wetlands support several species of frogs and salamanders, and caves near Narcisse and Inwood, in the Interlake region, have proved to be ideal hibernating areas for garter snakes. Their appearance in the thousands each spring has become a tourist attraction.

Because the province is so near the continent's geographical centre, the flight paths of many bird species converge here. Hawks,

Hiking path in La Barrière Park, just outside Winnipeg, on the banks of the La Salle River. *Inset:* Bald eagle.

owls, songbirds and grouse are common, as are geese, ducks and other waterfowl.

Manitoba's countless lakes and rivers teem with whitefish, pike, pickerel, lake trout and other species too numerous to mention. In fact, the province's three largest lakes are said to hold the richest variety of freshwater fish in North America.

The variety in Manitoba's natural vegetation is reflected in the mixture of plants that grow throughout the region. Plant life ranges from the willows, sedges, and lichens of the tundra to the cat-tails of the marshes and the aspen and oak trees of the parklands. The prairie grasslands are now mostly cultivated and are famous for their domestic grains, wheat, oats and barley and special crops such as flax and canola. Many wild grasses, flowers, and willows dominated the landscape in the past.

Climate

The climate for most of Manitoba hits extremes of hot and cold. In Winnipeg, average temperatures are -19.3° C (-2.7° F) in January

Left: Winter at the corner of Portage and Main. Winnipegers take pride in this corner's reputation as the coldest and windiest in North America. *Above:* Canoeing on the Bloodvein River in Atikaki Wilderness Park.

and 19.6° C (67.3° F) in July. At Churchill on the Hudson Bay coast, the average for January is -27.5° C (-17.5° F) and for July 11.8° C (52.3° F).

The amount of precipitation varies across the province, with the southeast receiving the most and the north receiving the least. Most of Southern Manitoba receives about 500 millimetres (20 inches) a year, almost two-thirds of it in the summer.

In terms of sunshine, Manitoba is one of North America's bright spots. Winnipeg enjoys more than 2000 hours of bright sunshine each year on average, and most of the rest of the province is just as sunny.

In the north, summer temperatures still do not venture far above those of the Ice Age. There, summers are so short that frost stays in the ground year-round. Only a shallow layer ever thaws. The frozen ground beneath is called permafrost. Permafrost poses special problems in construction. If heat from a building escapes into the ground, it can melt the permafrost, causing the foundation to sink and fill with water. Engineers face similar problems building highways, railroads and sewage disposal systems.

The flatlands of the south central region, including the Red River Valley, are flood-prone. Every few years, a fast snow melt or too much spring rain causes the rivers and streams to overflow their banks and flood the countryside.

The most widespread flood on record in the region took place in 1826, a few years after the Selkirk settlers arrived. But the most devastating flood in Manitoba's history — and perhaps Canada's —

During the disastrous 1950 flood, the Red River rose almost 10 m (33 ft.) above its normal level. Over 1550 km² (600 sq. mi.) of southern Manitoba were submerged, including 17 percent of the city of Winnipeg.

took place in the spring of 1950, when the Red River spilled over its banks and flooded a vast stretch of farmland, dozens of towns and villages and large parts of Winnipeg. Damage estimates at the time ranged as high as $100 million (which would be much higher in today's currency). About 100 000 people were forced out of their homes.

A floodway built in the 1960s now diverts excess waters of the Red River around Winnipeg. The 47.3-kilometre (29-mile) Red River Floodway was truly a world class engineering project. To create it, engineers moved half as much earth as was moved to build the Panama Canal. Since 1968, the floodway has proved its usefulness at least four times, especially in 1979 when the Red River reached levels similar to those of 1950. Other flood control projects include dikes around the towns along the Red River, and a diversion of the Assiniboine River to Lake Manitoba, just west of Portage la Prairie.

The Manitoba Floodway, which now diverts floodwaters around Winnipeg, is almost as wide as the Red River itself.

CHAPTER 3

The People

One of Manitoba's most popular festivals is Winnipeg's Folklorama. Each August for two weeks, halls, churches and community centres come alive with the colours, aromas and rhythms of distant lands as the city celebrates the diverse cultures of Manitoba's one million citizens. And Folklorama is just one of Manitoba's ethnic festivals. Every summer the town of Dauphin celebrates the National Ukrainian Festival and Gimli holds its Icelandic Festival. Steinbach honours its Mennonite roots and Thompson hosts Indian Days. St. Boniface celebrates the French-Canadian culture with the Festival du Voyageur each winter.

The First Manitobans

The earliest evidence that has been found indicates that there were people in what is now Manitoba between 10 000 and 15 000 years ago. At that time the great ice sheet that had covered the region was in full retreat, leaving behind a huge lake and extensive grasslands. Little is known about these early Manitobans, but it seems that they hunted the great plains bison and perhaps the mammoth.

By the time Europeans arrived in the area it had undergone many changes. The terrain was much as it is today, and several groups of natives lived in the region. Between Lake Superior and Lake Winnipeg were the Saulteaux, a tribe of Ojibwa Indians; farther north were the Cree, and still farther north, the Chipewyan; to the south were the Assiniboines. Each group had adapted to the resources of its environment and developed a distinctive way of life.

The first Europeans to arrive in Manitoba were headed by Captain Thomas Button, a British explorer, who wintered his two ships on the western shores of Hudson Bay in 1612. Like many other explorers of his day, he was looking for a route to the Far East and was not very interested in the land in which he found himself. He did, however, map this shallow inland sea and the rivers that emptied into it. He also gave Manitoba its first recorded name — New Wales. That name didn't stick, but another one of his choosing did: he named the Nelson River after his navigator, Francis Nelson, who died of scurvy that winter.

Over the next two centuries, English and French fur traders met, traded with, and were guided by natives throughout the region. Some married native women and the children of these marriages became the Métis, a new people who developed their own customs and way of life.

Exactly 200 years after Button's visit, a Scottish nobleman, Thomas Douglas, Earl of Selkirk, arranged for a group of Scottish tenant farmers to start farming along the banks of the Red and Assiniboine rivers. The Selkirk settlers were the first Europeans to try farming in this fertile but challenging region.

The Peopling of Manitoba

People trickled into Manitoba throughout the nineteenth century, but significant migration into the province began in the 1870s. In 1871 Manitoba's population stood at 25 000, but by 1891 it had grown to more than 150 000. Some of the newcomers were from Britain and Western Europe, but most were from Ontario where almost all the good farmland had been settled. There were also groups of German-speaking Mennonites who were fleeing religious persecution and Icelanders who had been forced out of their homeland by natural disasters.

Another wave of immigrants followed about fifteen years later, and by 1911 the population stood at 461 000. Many of these new settlers came from the United States, where good land had become expensive, and some still came from eastern Canada, Britain and

Left: The first Selkirk settlers arrive at Red River in August 1812. *Below:* Four Sisters of Charity, or Grey Nuns as they are usually called, arrive at Red River in 1844 to set up the colony's first hospital. *Bottom left:* A statue of a Viking ship honours the heritage of the Icelandic Settlers who first came to the shores of Lake Winnipeg in 1875. They named their landing site *Gimli*, which means "the great hall of heaven."

Western Europe. But these traditional sources could not provide enough settlers to fill the West. As a result, Clifford Sifton, the minister responsible for immigration after 1896, launched a campaign to attract peasants from central and eastern Europe. The response was all he could have hoped for. Between 1896 and 1914 more than 170 000 Ukrainian immigrants settled in Canada, many of them in Manitoba. Significant numbers of Poles, Jews and Russians also settled in the province during this period.

The First World War put an end to the immigration boom, except for colonies of Hutterites who came from the United States in 1918. Immigration picked up in the mid-twenties, only to be halted again by the Depression and the Second World War. In the late forties and early fifties, thousands of refugees from Europe's war-torn countries found a welcome in Manitoba.

In the 1970s and 1980s, a growing proportion of the newcomers came from the Caribbean, South and Central America, Africa and Asia. Many, like the Vietnamese, were refugees fleeing harsh regimes in their homelands. Refugees also came from parts of Latin America, including Chile, Nicaragua and El Salvador.

Manitoba Today

In terms of population, Manitoba ranks fifth among the provinces with slightly over a million people. More than half of them live in Winnipeg. In no other province is there such a huge gap between the population of the biggest city and that of the next biggest: about 650 000 people live in Winnipeg, more than sixteen times as many as in Brandon. Almost 40 000 Manitobans live in the other three cities — Thompson, Portage la Prairie and Flin Flon. The rest live in towns and villages or on farms or reserves.

Manitoba has about 72 000 Native Indians, two-thirds of whom live on about fifty reserves scattered across the province. Most of the others live in Winnipeg and other cities or in small northern communities.

Above left: **Pow-wow at Portage la Prairie.** *Above:* **Holy Trinity Ukrainian Orthodox Cathedral, Winnipeg.** *Left:* **Parade launching Winnipeg's two-week multicultural festival, Folklorama.**

Roman Catholics make up the largest single religious group in the province, with United Church members ranking a close second and Anglicans a more distant third. Given the cultural diversity of the people, it is not surprising that many other religions are represented in the province. In Winnipeg, in particular, the distinctive domed churches of Ukrainian Catholic and Greek Orthodox faiths mingle with synagogues, mosques and Buddhist, Hindu and Sikh temples.

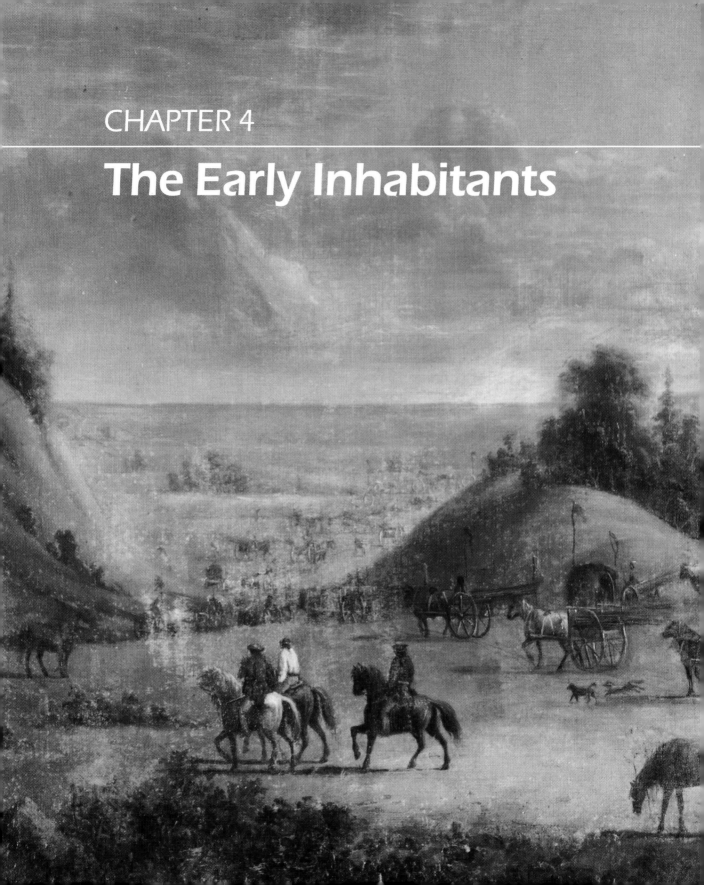

CHAPTER 4
The Early Inhabitants

In 1670, the Hudson's Bay Company was given a royal charter and the exclusive right to trade for furs with the natives in all of the lands whose rivers drained into Hudson Bay. The region was named Rupert's Land. Present-day Manitoba was only a small part of the total area, which included northern Quebec and Ontario, and parts of Saskatchewan and Alberta.

When the Europeans arrived, there were several native tribes occupying what is now Manitoba. Each had a formula for living well. The Assiniboine in the south depended primarily on the huge herds of bison that grazed on the prairies. Hunting at the time on foot (horses did not reach the Canadian plains until the mid-1700s), they stampeded the animals over the edge of cliffs or drove them into corrals. Many could be slaughtered at a time this way, providing the people with food, skins for clothing and shelter, bone and sinew for tools and utensils. In the forested areas of the southeast, the Saulteaux lived by hunting, fishing and harvesting wild rice. Their neighbours to the north, the Cree, also relied on hunting and fishing and gathered berries, nuts and other wild plants. The Chipewyans, in the barren lands that begin in northern Manitoba, depended on the caribou in much the same way as the Plains Indians based their economy on the bison.

Even before the Europeans arrived, the natives had longstanding trading patterns. They regularly exchanged hides and wild rice for corn from the people living farther south. There was also an active trade in handcrafted items.

Overleaf: The Métis buffalo hunt was a large, well-organized expedition. In June 1840, for example, the hunt involved 1210 carts and 1630 men, women and children.

Top left: After stampeding the buffalo over a cliff, native hunters killed the injured animals with stone-headed clubs or spears. *Lower left:* Saulteaux women harvested wild rice at the end of the summer, beating the kernels off the plants into the canoes. *Below:* Native encampment.

29

A Time of Change

As the fur trade expanded in the seventeenth and eighteenth centuries, European trading posts sprang up all through the region. The French, who had been trading furs for decades in eastern Canada, also came into the region. In the 1730s, La Vérendrye and his sons pushed west through the Great Lakes and the river system leading into Lake Winnipeg. They built forts on the Red and Assiniboine rivers, and other traders soon followed. At first, everyone gained from this exchange of goods. The Europeans got valuable furs in return for inexpensive metal pots and tools, guns, and other items. The natives acquired the products of an unknown technology in exchange for something commonplace for them — furs.

Not all of North America's natives lived close to European traders. Some of those who did became middlemen, specializing in trading furs for European goods, and then trading European goods to other natives — often for a good profit. They came to be known as the Home Guard Indians.

There were quite a few Home Guard Cree living close to one Hudson's Bay trading post, York Factory. In years when food was hard to get, they often helped the traders with the food that came from their hunting. Then, when their hunts failed, they would call upon the fur traders for help. In other words, the traders became part of the food exchange pattern that was normal in Indian culture.

During this time, it was common for French and English fur traders to take Indian women as wives. Often the Indian wives played a role that went far beyond companionship. They worked with their husbands, knew the transport routes, and were good at handling the skins. Many children were born of these unions. Over time, as their numbers grew, they came to be known as the Métis.

Gradually, the Métis developed their own way of life, different from that of both the Indians and the Europeans. In the south, they became noted for their highly organized annual buffalo hunts. Many established themselves on long, narrow strips of land along

Left: Cree hunter and family near York Factory. *Above:* Monument honouring explorer Pierre Gaultier de La Vérendrye, located in La Vérendrye Park in St. Boniface.

the Red and Assiniboine rivers. They farmed part-time and worked in the fur trade as interpreters or transporting supplies in their Red River carts.

As they grew away from both their Indian and European ances-tors, the Métis became a people not fully accepted by either group. At first this hardly mattered. In fact, it was a source of pride to the Métis. They called themselves the New Nation and felt they had taken the best from both European and native cultures. But it would later cause them many problems.

CHAPTER 5

How Manitoba Was Settled

Most people who come to Manitoba today arrive on highways from the east, west and south, or by air. But three centuries ago, when the first fur traders arrived, they used a very different route — through Hudson Bay.

York Factory

The first place the Hudson's Bay Company set up shop was on a forlorn piece of Hudson Bay coast it named York Factory. York Factory was built in 1682 on a point of land between the mouths of the Hayes and Nelson rivers. Furs from the far western reaches of Rupert's Land could be brought there by canoe. Then ocean-going ships carried them to England.

Soon afterwards, the company built Fort Prince of Wales at the mouth of the Churchill River. In the years that followed, many other fortified trading posts were built throughout Rupert's Land.

To the Hudson's Bay Company, armed as it was with a royal charter and exclusive trading rights, the future seemed assured. But the fur trade was a complex business, and international events made it even more complex.

England and France were involved in a series of wars over who would own the colonies in the New World and elsewhere. Despite their forbidding locations, the Hudson Bay posts were worth fighting over. During the late 1600s and the early 1700s, Fort Prince of Wales changed hands several times. From 1694 to 1713, York Factory was occupied by the French.

A view of Upper Fort Garry.

York Factory in its heyday. *Inset:* The partly restored Fort Prince of Wales at the mouth of the Churchill River is now a National Historic Park.

For about 150 years, York Factory was the busiest fur trading post in Western Canada. But as a place to live, it left a lot to be desired. It was freezing cold in winter and infested with biting insects in summer. Still, life there was better than the one many of the people who worked there had left behind in England or Europe. Aside from busy times, such as when the yearly supply ship arrived, they had time to pursue hobbies. There was lots of wildlife, and they could hunt and fish. Besides, a job at York Factory offered ordinary people a rare chance for a better life. Many workers saved more than half of their pay and returned home in fifteen or twenty years with several hundred pounds. That was a respectable fortune, enough to buy a farm or small business.

York Factory reached its peak of activity around 1840. With forty to fifty employees stationed at the site, trappers coming and going, workers' families and company contractors, it was a busy community. Before long, however, other trade routes began diverting traffic to the south. Railroads were being built across the United States in the 1840s, and steamers began plying the Red River in the 1860s. There were other, cheaper ways to ship furs, and York Factory declined in importance though it was not officially closed until 1957. Since 1968 it has been a national historic site.

Manitoba's Beginnings

In 1800, the rivalry between the Hudson's Bay Company and the North West Company was at its peak. The Nor'Westers were established at Fort Gibraltar, near the Forks, and many of the Métis of the area made their living supplying and transporting provisions for them.

A series of events began in 1811 that threatened both the commerce of the North West Company and the Métis' way of life. That year, Thomas Douglas, fifth Earl of Selkirk, persuaded the Hudson's Bay Company to grant him a large tract of land. Assiniboia, as it was called, included the Red and Assiniboine river valleys and stretched westward into Saskatchewan and southward into the United States. At the time many small tenant farmers, or crofters, were being forced off their land in Scotland to make way for large-scale sheep farming. Lord Selkirk wanted to help them settle in the New World.

Led by a retired soldier, Miles Macdonell, the first group of thirty-six settlers arrived in York Factory in the fall of 1811. It was too late in the year to go farther, so they spent the winter in hastily-made huts near the Hudson Bay coast. They reached the Forks the following August. With the help of a band of Saulteaux Indians led by Chief Peguis, they built Fort Douglas and planted a crop of winter wheat before the snow fell. Another group of seventy-one settlers joined them in October, and a third group arrived in 1814.

Two Great Companies

In 1713, the French acknowledged once and for all English claim to Rupert's Land. But this official act did not stop LaVérendrye and later traders from using the Great Lakes route and establishing inland posts. Rupert's Land was simply too big for the Hudson's Bay Company to patrol.

The *voyageurs* from New France had advantages. They lived off the land, and did not have to carry all their provisions. They travelled to the Indian villages to trade, instead of waiting for the Indians to come to their posts.

Even the withdrawal of France from North America after the Seven Years War did not mean the end of competition for the Hudson's Bay Company. In fact, the competition grew worse as a number of merchants based in Montreal financed trading expeditions along the old French route.

Left: **Red River guide.** *Below:* **The Red River colony as sketched by Lord Selkirk in 1817.**

In 1784, most of the Montreal merchants joined together to form the North West Company. For the next thirty years their traders were often able to outhustle the Hudson's Bay traders. But the long-term advantage lay with the older company because of its faster and cheaper route into the heart of the continent. In 1821 the North West Company merged with the Hudson's Bay Company to create a real fur trading monopoly.

The Selkirk settlers came with the blessing of the Hudson's Bay Company, but the Nor'Westers and the Métis saw them as intruders who threatened their business and their way of life. Lord Selkirk might have given Governor Macdonell authority, but none of those who were already there would take orders from this newcomer.

Macdonell's authority was first tested in 1814, when an early frost severely damaged the crops. Fearing famine in the colony, he decreed that no food could be taken out of Assiniboia for a year. His order made sense to the settlers, but it angered others. Each year the Nor'Westers sent pemmican — dried buffalo meat or venison provided by the Métis — out of the region to feed their canoeists on the long journey to and from the company's far-flung western posts.

The Nor'Westers took the law into their own hands, arresting Macdonell and destroying Fort Douglas and the settlement. The settlers rebuilt, but the hostility was to get worse. In 1816 a group of Métis, encouraged by the Nor'Westers and led by Cuthbert Grant set out to attack the settlement and force out the colonists once and for all. As they approached Fort Douglas, the new governor, Robert Semple, and twenty-seven men rode out to meet them. In the skirmish that followed near a grove of trees known as Seven Oaks, Semple and twenty of his men were killed, along with one of Grant's men.

The settlement was strengthened the following year when Lord Selkirk brought in a group of disbanded Swiss soldiers of the des Meurons regiment who had fought in the War of 1812. After that,

This winter scene shows ice fishing and a variety of other activities at the junction of the Red and Assiniboine rivers. It was painted by Peter Rindisbacher, a young artist who came from Switzerland with his family to settle at Red River.

an uneasy peace reigned in the Red River colony until 1821, when the merger of the North West and Hudson's Bay companies put an end to the fur-trade rivalry.

Many of the settlement's conflicts were resolved as a result of the merger, but not all the changes it brought about were positive. The rivalry had been expensive and now the governor of the Hudson's Bay Company, George Simpson, moved to cut costs. One result was fewer jobs, and many casual employees, especially the Métis from around Red River, found themselves without work.

Even so, the colony's population continued to grow. Some officers who retired from the companies chose to stay at Red River. After 1818, when the Canada-U.S. border was established along the 49th parallel in the West, many Métis who had lived south of the

The church and school established in the 1820s by Reverend John West, the first Anglican missionary at Red River.

border moved north. For years to come, the Métis would outnumber all of the other settlers around the Forks.

In 1834, Lord Selkirk's estate gave control of Assiniboia back to the Hudson's Bay Company. This assured the future of the colony as the company decided to develop it as a supply centre for the fur trade. There were other problems — frost, grasshoppers, drought and other natural disasters — but after a quarter of a century, the economic base of the settlement had been established.

CHAPTER 6

A New Province Is Forged

After 1850, it became clear that the Hudson's Bay Company could no longer govern Rupert's Land. The region was too big — almost half of present-day Canada — and fur trade profits were too small. As settlers drifted into the Red River region looking for farmland to settle, the tasks of administration got ever more time-consuming. Something had to change.

In 1867, four of the eastern provinces of British North America joined together to form the Dominion of Canada. Expansion westward was part of the new country's agenda. Not only was land needed for the growing population, but the government was nervous about the United States. If the West remained sparsely populated, might the Americans decide to expand northward? They had acquired a vast territory in wars with Mexico, and the Union Army had shown the power of its war machine during the Civil War in the 1860s.

The Hudson's Bay Company and the new nation of Canada struck a deal soon after Confederation. The company would hand over Rupert's Land to the Canadian government. In return, the government would pay the company £300,000 and give it one-seventh of the land in the "fertile belt" between the Red River and the Rockies — about 2.8 million hectares (6.9 million acres). Then Canada would annex the entire region and call it the North-West Territories.

Everyone was pleased with the arrangement — everyone, that

After the legislation that created the Province of Manitoba was passed, the Canadian government sent a military force to Red River to ensure order. The troops, led by Colonel Garnet Wolseley, are seen here beginning one of the 47 portages that had to be made between Lake Superior and the colony.

Métis farm at Red River. Seen in the foreground is one of the famous Red River carts. A Métis creation, these carts were made entirely of wood and could be taken apart and rowed across a river when necessary.

is, except the 10 000 or so Métis who lived in the Red River Settlement. Most of the new settlers made it clear that they looked down on the Métis and their way of life. The Métis feared the Canadian takeover would bring in more settlers who would drive away the bison and take their lands. Few of the Métis had actual legal title to their long narrow lots — they just held them through an informal agreement with the Hudson's Bay Company.

When a survey crew arrived during the summer of 1869 to mark off the boundaries from the Red River to Lake of the Woods for townships, the Métis saw it as a confirmation of their worst fears. They decided to make a stand for their rights, and in October, they forced the survey crew to stop work.

There was another touchy issue. To the Canadian government, William McDougall seemed like a logical person to appoint as the first governor of the new territory since he had taken part in negotiating the agreement with the Hudson's Bay Company. But the

Louis Riel (seated, centre) and his council.

Métis did not trust him, and when he arrived, a group of them took him across the U.S. border into Dakota Territory and told him to stay there. When he tried to cross into Canada again, he was escorted back again.

During these skirmishes, the Métis were led by Louis Riel, a brilliant young man who had studied in Montreal. Riel wanted to negotiate the terms of union with Canada, but he realized that he would have to have control of the colony before the government would take him seriously. So, late in the fall of 1869, he seized Fort Garry and proclaimed a provisional government.

The new government set itself the tasks of maintaining law and order and drawing up a list of demands. These included full provincial status for Manitoba, the freedom to educate the new province's children as Catholics in the French language, and land rights for the Métis.

Reluctantly, the federal government agreed to negotiate. Riel formed a committee of both English- and French-speaking citizens, and delegates were appointed to carry out the negotiations. Some of the people of Red River — especially those from Ontario — were unhappy with the things Riel was trying to do. They plotted to overthrow his provisional government but succeeded only in getting several of their number arrested.

One of Riel's most troublesome opponents was Thomas Scott, an Irishman from Ontario, who had nothing but contempt for Riel and the Métis community. After several arrests, a court-martial tribunal organized by the Métis sentenced Scott to death for insubordination. For whatever reason — perhaps he did not want to appear weak to the federal government — Riel allowed the sentence to stand, and on March 4, 1870, a firing squad executed Scott.

That was the turning point for Riel. The English-speaking community in Manitoba — and back in Ontario — saw Scott as a martyr. They were determined to have revenge and eventually succeeded in having a warrant issued for Riel's arrest. Nonetheless, Riel and his Métis followers had set the stage for negotiations between Canada and the Red River settlers, and on July 15, 1870, Manitoba joined Confederation as a province.

Shortly afterwards a miliary force headed for Manitoba to ensure order. Many of the volunteers were Ontarians determined to avenge Scott. Riel wisely fled to the United States before they arrived. Years later, he would return to Canada to lead the Métis of Saskatchewan in the Northwest Rebellion. After the rebellion was put down, Riel was arrested, tried for treason and hanged.

Although the Métis had got the guarantees they asked for, things did not work out as they had hoped. There were endless delays in turning over the land that had been promised them. Many left — tired of waiting or simply unable or unwilling to adjust to the changes created by large numbers of new settlers. Those who remained soon found themselves a small minority, treated as outsiders in their land.

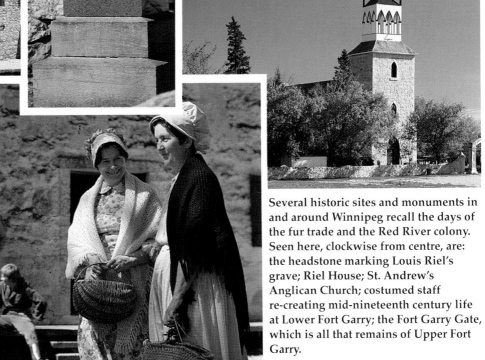

Several historic sites and monuments in and around Winnipeg recall the days of the fur trade and the Red River colony. Seen here, clockwise from centre, are: the headstone marking Louis Riel's grave; Riel House; St. Andrew's Anglican Church; costumed staff re-creating mid-nineteenth century life at Lower Fort Garry; the Fort Garry Gate, which is all that remains of Upper Fort Garry.

CHAPTER 7

The Young Province

Anyone familiar with the map of present-day Manitoba can be forgiven for not recognizing the province that came into being in 1870. The original Manitoba was so small — less than 10 000 square kilometres (3860 square miles) — it was often referred to as the postage-stamp province. As well, the Manitoba Act, the law that created the province, stated clearly that control of the land and natural resources was withheld "for the purposes of the Dominion." Not until the 1930s would Manitoba get control of its own resources.

The province was expanded twice — in 1881, to include new farm settlements, and in 1912 to give Manitoba the same northern boundary (the 60th parallel) as Alberta and Saskatchewan. Starting in 1871, and at various later times as the province expanded, treaties were signed with the Indians of the different regions. The Indians gave up their general rights to the land in return for reserves set aside for their sole use and certain other benefits.

Manitoba's Railway Boom

Winnipeg got a boost in 1870 when it was chosen as the capital of both Manitoba and the North-West Territories. Located halfway between Lake Winnipeg and the U.S. border, it was in a good position to provide many of the services needed in the Territories — shipping, warehousing, outfitting, retailing, financing, hotels and meals, and care for horses and livestock that passed through.

Abandoned farmhouses like this one may have been left behind when settlers moved on because their land proved too poor for successful farming. Some, on the other hand, are evidence of success — abandoned when the family could afford something bigger and better.

All through the 1870s there was talk of a transcontinental railway and even some construction. But there were many problems and delays, and by the time the line reached Manitoba, Winnipegers were ready to make a strong bid to have it pass through their city.

There were sound engineering reasons why the Canadian Pacific Railway (CPR) should have bypassed Winnipeg in favor of Selkirk, 30 kilometres (19 miles) to the north. The banks of the Red River were high at Selkirk, and the town was safe from spring flooding. Besides, the line was built almost to Selkirk by the time the serious bidding started.

However, Winnipeg businessmen and officials approached the CPR managers with an attractive offer: they promised to build the needed railway bridge across the Red River at their own expense and not to charge taxes, ever, on city land through which the line passed. The CPR found the offer irresistible, and the main line came through Winnipeg. One result was that speculators who had bought land in Selkirk in hopes of seeing its value go up were disappointed. Another was a short but spectacular land boom in Winnipeg.

By far the most dramatic phase of the city's growth took place in those early days when it was a railway construction town. In 1881 and 1882 property values rose to levels not seen again for a century. Like most land booms, the one in Winnipeg made many ordinary people very rich. And, in typical fashion, most of those who made fortunes in the early days of the buying frenzy became losers in the end. They borrowed more money to increase their fortunes further, only to see land values drop.

Winnipeg's gains were the most spectacular in Manitoba, but the price of land increased sharply in Portage la Prairie, Brandon and other towns along the CPR main line. Farm lands located near the railway rose in value too. There were reports of people who had made $100 000 or more from real estate dealings — and that at a time when $1200 a year was considered a good wage.

The boom lasted from mid-1881 until the spring of 1882. Real estate fortunes were made and lost, but Winnipeg's future as a major transport centre was assured. And there were many wise business-men who made lasting fortunes from the emerging business opportunities. A 1910 newspaper report listed nineteen Winnipeg millionaires. These included men like grain merchant Nicholas Bawlf, newspaper publisher and politician Clifford Sifton; financial broker A.M. Nanton; hardware merchant James Ashdown; and transportation and banking magnate William Alloway. By 1913 Winnipeg was Canada's third largest city, with 150 000 residents.

The difference 20 years or so can make: at left is the corner of Portage and Main in 1872; below, the same corner in 1894.

Growth 1896 - 1914

The coming of the railway in the 1880s set the stage for dramatic growth not only in Manitoba but right across the West. When the western United States, Britain and western Europe failed to produce enough immigrants to fill the prairies, Clifford Sifton, the minister responsible for immigration after 1896, ran advertising

Above: The long wearying job of clearing and breaking the land.
Left: Ukrainian settlers at Vita plaster the walls of their log house with clay, which they will then lime-wash to a dazzling whiteness.

campaigns in central and eastern Europe. Many of the claims about the fertility of the land were exaggerated, but they attracted thousands of people to settle on the prairies. For many ambitious people, prospects at home were so limited that even the harsh realities of climate, insects and drought seemed better. The land cost little or nothing, and the Canadian government paid most of the travel costs for immigrants and their families.

Below: **The French community of St. Claude celebrates Corpus Christi Sunday, 1910.**
Right: **Icelandic pioneers in the Gimli area about 1910.**

During its first forty years or so, Manitoba expanded rapidly. As the settlements spread throughout the province, the CPR built branch lines, so that almost all of the farming areas had easy access to rail service. As the number of people in the West increased, so did the demand for goods and services. Winnipeg became the main depot for a variety of goods shipped from eastern Canada. It also became a key manufacturing centre, competing with Montreal firms in areas such as clothing and furniture.

The Grain Trade

Winnipeg's location as the point through which all grain had to pass, whether heading to eastern Canada or overseas, made it a logical gathering place for grain merchants, shippers, exporters and suppliers.

In 1887, several Winnipeg grain traders decided to set up a central marketplace in which to buy and sell grain and to arrange for grading, storage, shipping and other aspects of the trade.

They organized the Winnipeg Grain and Produce Exchange, later known as the Winnipeg Grain Exchange and then The Winnipeg Commodity Exchange. In the early years of this century, it was one of the world's main grain trading centres. Wheat prices at the Winnipeg Grain Exchange set the pace for the rest of the world. Today Winnipeg is still an important grain centre, and grain merchants still buy and sell grain at the exchange.

Some farmers didn't like the way grain prices were set on the Winnipeg Grain Exchange. Although it was never proven, they were convinced the markets were rigged to benefit grain merchants at the expense of producers. By the 1920s farmers were so dissatisfied with the system that they set up a series of grain marketing co-operatives. By then they had also formed their own political party, the United Farmers of Manitoba. They sent twelve members to the legislature in 1920 and formed the government in 1922.

The Manitoba Schools Question

One of the most bitter French-English controversies in Canadian history began about a century ago in Manitoba.

To satisfy Métis demands, English and French were declared the official languages of the government and courts by the Manitoba Act of 1870. There were also provisions for government support of both Catholic and Protestant schools, and no restrictions on the language of instruction.

In 1871 the Manitoba Legislature set up a dual school system as provided for in the act. Since Roman Catholics tended to speak French and Protestants tended to be English-speaking, the language of instruction in Catholic schools was usually French, in Protestant schools it was English.

In 1870, there were about the same number of French-Catholic families and English-Protestant families in the province. Twenty years later, however, there had been a dramatic change. By 1890, English-speaking families made up about 80 percent of the total, as most of the immigrants at the time were Protestant Europeans, Britons and Americans.

A typical early school in rural Manitoba.

In 1890, the Legislative Assembly passed two new laws that reflected this population shift. One was the Official Language Act, which made English the official language in Manitoba. The other was the Public Schools Act. It withdrew public support from Catholic schools by setting up a non-denominational school system. Catholics could organize private schools at their own expense, but their property taxes would still support the public school system.

The French-speaking minority felt angry and betrayed, particularly by the school act. They appealed it all the way to the Privy Council in London. This body upheld the act — but added that the federal government could intervene to restore a right a minority had had on entering Confederation.

The Manitoba Schools Question thus became a national issue — one of the issues on which Wilfrid Laurier and his Liberals fought and won the 1896 federal election.

As prime minister, Laurier worked out a compromise with Manitoba Premier Thomas Greenway. The most important concession to the French-speaking minority allowed teaching in a language other than English — French or any other minority language — under certain conditions. The main condition was that a minimum number of students was available to learn in the minority language.

No one was very enthusiastic about the compromise, but it worked quite well for a while. Then came the influx of immigrants whose language was neither French nor English. There was no way the government could meet their requests for trained teachers who could teach in their various languages, and in 1916, the Manitoba government abolished the "bilingual clause." It would be more than fifty years before French instruction was formally restored in the province.

Women's Struggle for the Vote

Early in the twentieth century, many women across Canada, in the U.S. and England were engaged in a battle to be recognized as the

Members of the Manitoba Political Equality League and their petition demanding the vote for women. On the right in front is Amelia Burritt who at the age of 94 collected over 4000 signatures.

intellectual and social equals of men. One of the first issues to be tackled on the road to equality was the law that allowed only men to vote.

In Manitoba, the struggle was led by women from the Icelandic community and the members of the Women's Christian Temperance Union. Among the most active members of the WCTU were Mrs. M.J. Benedictssen, Lillian Benyon Thomas, Dr. Amelia Yeomans, Cora Hind and Nellie McClung. In 1912, these women formed the Political Equality League and began an all-out campaign to pressure the Manitoba government to extend voting rights to women. They produced pamphlets, wrote newspaper articles and collected thousands of signatures on petitions. One of their most effective tactics was the staging of a Mock Parliament. Nellie McClung as premier wittily demonstrated the absurdity of the arguments against women voting by using them to explain why it would be wrong to allow men to vote.

It took a change of government and a petition with over 40 000 signatures, but on January 28, 1916, Manitoba women became the first in Canada to gain the right to vote in a provincial election and to hold elected public office.

CHAPTER 8
New Challenges

The early years of the twentieth century were a good time for Manitoba. The farm economy prospered and Winnipeg continued to grow as a retail, agriculture and transportation centre.

Then almost as suddenly as they began, the good times were over. Wheat prices fell in 1912 and 1913, and investment money dried up. To make matters worse, the Panama Canal was due to open in the fall of 1914. It would mean that goods could be moved between eastern and western Canada more cheaply by sea than overland. Winnipeg's position as gateway to the West was threatened. Before that threat became a reality, however, the country was at war.

An incredible number of Manitobans — more than 65 000 out of a population of fewer than 500 000 — joined the armed forces during the First World War. Of these, more than 7800 were killed in action. There were 70 dead from the village of Killarney, 55 from Gladstone, 122 from Neepawa.

When it was discovered that three winners of the Victoria Cross — the highest award for valour in the British Empire — had lived on Pine Street in Winnipeg's West End, the street name was changed to Valour Road. The three were Sergeant Frederick Hall and Sergeant Leo Clark, whose heroism cost them their lives, and Captain Robert Shankland.

With the outbreak of the war came increased demand for all kinds of goods. Most prices rose quickly in Canada, as elsewhere. One exception was grain. The federal government clamped a ceiling

Colourful farm fields near Teulon. The bright yellow field is canola in flower, the bluish ones are flax.

All People's Mission was founded by the Methodist Church to help the thousands of poor immigrants who lived in appalling conditions in the slums of Winnipeg's North End. The mission ran a kindergarten, gave English lessons and distributed food and clothing to those in greatest need.

on grain prices in order to ensure reasonably priced food supplies for its European allies. Nothing stopped farmers' costs from going up though, and this dampened prosperity in the province.

Something else that did not go up was the wages employers paid their workers. Most wage labourers, many of them immigrants, worked long hours for little pay. In some cases they worked seven days a week, twelve hours a day, in dismal and sometimes unsafe conditions.

After the war ended in 1918, world demand for goods and services suffered a sharp and sudden drop. The number of jobs in Manitoba and elsewhere was decreasing just as the soldiers were returning from Europe. Unemployment became a serious problem. The frustrations of the workers simmered all though the winter of 1918-19. They boiled over on May 15, 1919, in the Winnipeg General Strike.

In March of that year, a group of western delegates attended a meeting of the Trades and Labour Congress in Calgary and were present at the birth of One Big Union (OBU). The idea behind the OBU was that a single, large union would be able to force employers to give workers a better deal where small, single-trade unions had failed. Talk at the meeting was occasionally extreme: greetings were sent to Russian revolutionaries and a general strike was threatened.

The Winnipeg General Strike began after talks between union and management in the building and metal trades broke down in early May. Union demands included better wages and working conditions, as well as acceptance of the principle of collective bargaining.

When the call for a general strike went out on May 15, the response was overwhelming. Within a few hours, some 30 000 workers had left their jobs — almost the entire work force. About one-third of the strikers were not even union members. All but essential services were stopped. The Workers' Central Strike Committee organized bread and milk delivery and made sure that water, electricity and police services were provided. People rushed to the stores with suitcases to buy food. Meat spoiled when the weather turned hot and there was a shortage of ice. Mountains of garbage piled up.

Neither the business owners nor officials from any level of government — civic, provincial or federal — tried to address the strikers' complaints. The OBU was not yet fully organized, but some of its planners were involved in the Winnipeg Strike. Employers and other influential Canadians were convinced that the strike leaders intended to overthrow the government. They formed a Citizens' Committee of 1000 to oppose the strike.

Federal politicians such as the acting Minister of Justice, Arthur Meighen, supported the Citizens' Committee. The government even amended the Immigration Act so that any foreign-born immigrant — including the British-born who were automatically Canadian citizens — could be deemed a troublemaker and deported without trial.

By mid-June, the strike was obviously failing and penniless

Troops at Portage and Main following the "Bloody Saturday" protest during the Winnipeg General Strike.

workers were trickling back to their jobs. The end did not come fast enough for the government, however. On June 17, ten strike leaders were arrested. When strikers and sympathizers gathered on June 21, "Bloody Saturday," to protest, a squadron of Royal North-West Mounted Police, armed with rifles and baseball bats, charged into the crowd. Dozens of people were injured and two died.

In the end, the strikers were defeated, and the last of them returned to their jobs on June 26. Among those arrested was OBU leader R.B. (Bob) Russell. Another strike supporter, James S. Woodsworth was arrested and charged but never brought to trial. In the next federal election, he ran for Parliament and won, holding his seat until his death in 1942. A commission appointed to look into the strike concluded that the strikers had genuine grievances caused by poor pay and working conditions.

The Great Depression

Prosperity returned to Manitoba during the 1920s, and before the decade was out, the value of industrial production had exceeded that of agriculture. During the 1920s power plants were built, the copper and zinc mining town of Flin Flon was founded and the province's first paper mill was opened at Pine Falls. A rail link with Hudson Bay, first proposed in 1880 and under construction off and on since 1906, was finally completed.

Manitoba joined Canada and the rest of the world in suffering through the Great Depression of the 1930s. The collapse in world trade meant that products made for export, including grain and resources industries were among the hardest hit. The effect of the collapse of grain prices was made even worse by the drought of the mid-1930s. As unemployment levels rose to 20 percent or higher, farms were devastated by crop failures and low prices, and many firms went out of business altogether. The Great Depression affected all Manitobans.

Laying track on the Hudson Bay Railway line in the 1920s. *Inset:* **During the Great Depression of the 1930s farm people sometimes hitched their horses to the car they could no longer afford to run. The set-up was called a Bennett Buggy after Richard B. Bennett, who was prime minister from 1930 to 1935.**

War and the Postwar Years

After nearly a decade of depression, the world stumbled into another widespread conflict in 1939. Once again, Canadians took part in the war alongside the British and their allies. The losses were less severe than they had been in 1914-18, but nearly 4000 Manitobans died in the Second World War.

Generally speaking, the postwar years through the fifties and sixties were prosperous times for Manitoba, as they were for most of the country. With the arrival of refugees from Europe and the birth of the baby-boomers, the population grew faster than it had for decades. Suburbs sprawled out from the cities in all directions. Schools and shopping malls multiplied. Brandon College and United College became universities, cultural institutions blossomed and Winnipeg got its first skyscraper.

In 1962, Winnipeg's famous "gingerbread" City Hall went under the wrecker's ball to make room for the sleek, modern building seen on the right.

Issues Old and New

One of the longest-running controversies in Manitoba was created by the development of the province's huge hydro–electric potential. From the political wrangling over the contract to develop the Seven Sisters Falls power site in the 1920s to the rerouting of part of the Churchill River into the Nelson system in the 1970s, there have been constant complaints about the financial, social and environmental management of this great resource.

The Nelson River development caused particular problems because it meant the flooding of vast areas of northern land and disrupted the traditional lifestyles of many native people. In 1977, the provincial and federal governments signed the Northern Flood Agreement with northern natives, assuring them that they would be repaid for damage to their property and interruptions to their traditional lifestyle.

But the native people complained the terms of the agreement were never honoured. In 1992, the five bands affected started to negotiate a series of settlements that would resolve the issues for cash payments and land grants. By 1996, all had agreed at least in principle to the terms.

In 1979, the French-English language issue again received national attention when a St. Boniface businessman refused to pay a parking fine because it was written in English only. He took his case to the Supreme Court of Canada and won. Then in 1985, the Supreme Court ruled that under the Manitoba Act, the province's laws must be published in both English and French. This meant that none of the laws enacted since 1890 were valid because they were published only in English. The court gave the province several years to translate its statutes.

On the economic front, providing services had become more important by the late 1980s than agriculture and manufacturing combined. Manitobans have developed expertise in many fields —

Bright red farm buildings like these at Strathclair are seen throughout southern Manitoba.

including medical research, computer technology, financial services and the aerospace industry. Even so, Manitobans are still looking for ways to cope with the diminishing role of primary products in the economy. Ideally, some of the new industries would be located in smaller communities. This would help slow the decades-long trend away from farms and smaller centres.

This trend has speeded up as a result of the low farm prices that have prevailed in recent years. The continent-wide farm crisis of the 1980s hit the province's farmers hard. Thousands were forced into bankruptcy. Others became so discouraged they sold their land and found another way of life. Some of those who left had been farming land their grandparents had settled a century ago.

Some of the issues that preoccupied all Canadians in the late eighties and early nineties had particular meaning in Manitoba. It was Elijah Harper, a native member of the Legislature, who prevented the province from ratifying the constitutional package known as the Meech Lake Accord in June 1990. His stand forced the provinces and the federal government to develop new constitutional initiatives to present to Canadians. At about the same time, an inquiry into how the justice system has served the province's native people obliged Manitobans to face the fact that serious changes were needed not only to practices but to attitudes.

About 3000 Cree live on the Cross Lake Reserve, north of Lake Winnipeg. The lake itself is an island-studded expansion of the Nelson River.

In connection with another major issue, Manitoba has taken a leading role in trying to integrate economic development with environmental renewal. Since it came into being in 1989, the Manitoba Round Table on Environment and Economy, a committee of politicians, business people and ordinary citizens has defined "sustainable development" for the province, set guidelines and embarked on a wide-ranging program to further the cause of sustainable development. Nonetheless, concerns about the environment continue to emerge. A variety of recent development projects aroused the opposition of environmentalists and concern continues about the effects of flooding parts of northern Manitoba to add to Manitoba Hydro's generating potential.

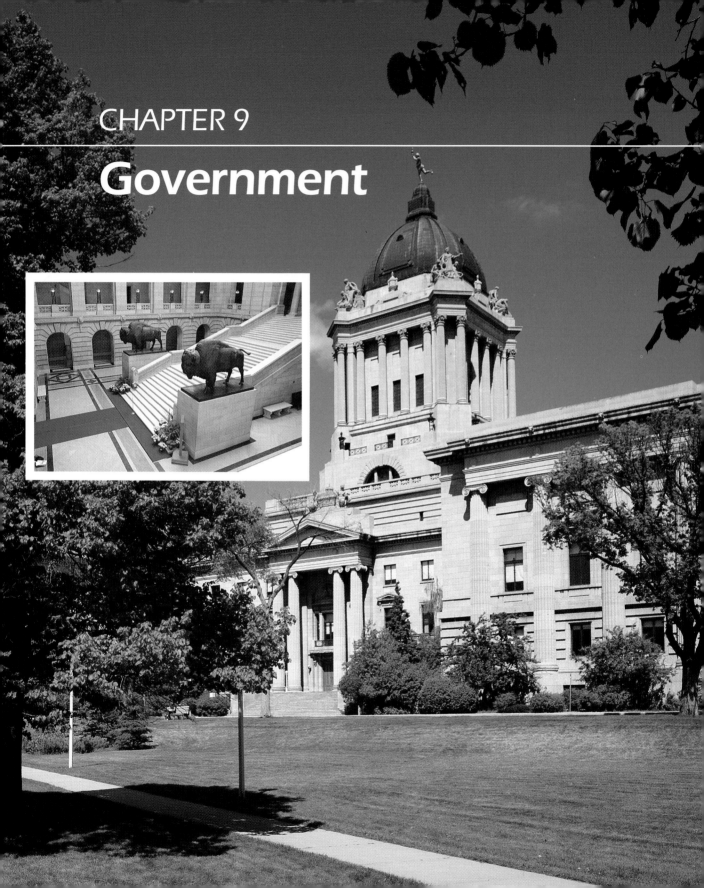

CHAPTER 9

Government

The Manitoba Act, which made Manitoba the first non-founding province to join Confederation, received Royal Assent on May 12, 1870. It came into effect two months later and Manitoba's first legislature was opened on March 15, 1871.

Manitoba's government, like that of all the provinces, is based on the British parliamentary model. It includes a lieutenant-governor who is the Queen's official representative and a governing body elected from fifty-seven legislative constituencies. Each constituency, or riding, elects one member of the Legislative Assembly. Together, these members (MLAs) represent all the people of the province.

Manitoba has a unicameral system, that is, just one level of Parliament — no Senate as in Ottawa, or Upper House as in the British Parliament. The task of the legislature is to pass the laws that govern the province. It has the right to tax its citizens, to finance the political system and carry out its policies and programs. An election is held whenever the first minister, or premier, chooses to call one, but elections cannot be more than five years apart. To call an election, the premier asks the lieutenant-governor to dissolve the legislature.

Canada's three major parties — The Progressive Conservative party, the New Democratic party and the Liberal party — dominate Manitoba's political life. In most cases, the party with the greatest number of MLAs forms the government. Usually, but not always, this party controls more than half of the seats in the legislature.

The Manitoba Legislative Building, Winnipeg. *Inset:* A pair of bronze bison stand watch over the building's magnificent lobby.

Government House, the residence of the lieutenant-governor is located on the grounds of the Legislative Building. Also on the grounds are several statues honouring major historical figures, including heroes of the province's ethnic communities such as Ukrainian poet Taras Shevchenko.

In 1995, the Progressive Conservatives were re-elected under their leader, Premier Gary Filmon. Filmon first came to power in 1988, when he replaced Howard Pawley, a New Democrat. The Liberals haven't been in power in Manitoba since 1958, when the last Liberal-Progressive coalition was dissolved.

The premier chooses his cabinet from the elected members of his party. The cabinet is a kind of management committee, and most of its members head one or more government departments.

Most legislative bills pass to "committee stage" at some point in the political process. This is when members of the public, corporations and interested groups usually have a chance to present their views to a standing committee of the legislature. Their presentation, which may be short or very long, is called a brief. Briefs may take a strong stand for or against the bill being considered, or may simply make practical suggestions to improve the legislation.

The provincial government delivers a wide variety of services to Manitoba citizens. Some are paid for in conjunction with the federal government, while others are financed completely by the province. Manitobans receive health care and welfare services through the provincial system, but the federal government covers some of the cost through transfer payments, as it does across Canada. Other services delivered by the provincial system include higher education, legal services, most highways and transport services, and some public utilities, such as electricity and telephones.

The province also cost-shares some programs that are delivered by the municipalities. Examples of this include the public school system and the municipal roads programs.

Other Levels of Government

The provincial government does not govern all aspects of political life.

Fourteen Members of Parliament and six Senators represent the interests of Manitobans at the federal level. In addition, there is a federal-provincial process, in which cabinet ministers from Manitoba and the other provinces meet, exchange views and interact with the federal government.

There are five types of local government, consisting of the governments of Manitoba's 5 incorporated cities, 35 incorporated towns, 39 incorporated villages, 105 rural municipalities and 17 local government districts. These governments have certain powers of taxation, and they control programs such as fire-fighting and maintaining municipal roads.

The provincial Department of Northern Affairs governs most of the few areas not organized as local government districts.

The Court System

The province's senior court is the Manitoba Court of Appeal. It is made up of a chief justice and six other judges. All are appointed by the federal government. A panel of three or five judges (always odd-numbered so that decisions do not end in a tie) hear arguments in cases where the prosecution or the defense is not satisfied with the decisions rendered in lower courts. Only the Supreme Court of Canada can reverse this court's decisions.

The highest trial court is the Court of Queen's Bench. It has a chief justice, an associate chief justice, and several other judges, all federally appointed. This court rules on civil lawsuits as well as most criminal cases, and it administers a Small Claims Court, where claims of up to $3000 are heard.

The Provincial Court has jurisdiction on most other matters under the Criminal Code and on most provincial issues. Provincial Court judges sit in nineteen permanent locations and in fifty-four temporary "circuit" locations around the province. The court has a Family Division and a Youth Court, where cases involving persons under eighteen are heard.

Education

Each of Manitoba's forty-seven school divisions is administered by an elected school board. There are also ten school districts under the control of the province. In 1992 there were just under 200 000 students enrolled in the province. Serving these students were approximately 15 000 teachers.

Elementary school consists of kindergarten through grade 8. The senior, or high school program, grades 9 through 12, includes several optional courses in addition to a core curriculum. Some schools offer vocational-industrial and vocational-business training. In addition, the province has schools for the disabled, the blind, the deaf, and those with learning disabilities.

The Administration
Building of the
University of
Manitoba.

It hasn't always been so, but today Manitobans can be educated
in either French or English. In addition, there are a number of heritage language programs, under which students may be educated in
German, Ukrainian or some other language, provided that the
school meets provincial standards.

More advanced career training is provided at three community
colleges — Red River Community College in Winnipeg, Assiniboine Community College in Brandon and Keewatin Community
College in The Pas.

There are three universities — The University of Manitoba, the
University of Winnipeg and Brandon University. Affiliated with the
University of Manitoba are St. John's College, associated with the
Anglican Church of Canada; St. Paul's College, associated with the
Roman Catholic Church; University College; and St. Boniface Col-
lege, where courses are delivered in French. The University of
Winnipeg grew out of United College, which was associated with
the United Church of Canada.

CHAPTER 10

The Economy

DAUPHIN

The extent to which Manitoba's economy has changed is well illustrated by the role of the area's first commercial industry, the fur trade. Once the mainstay of the region's economy, the fur trade today makes up only a tiny part of the total activity. In 1995-96, the province's 8500 trappers earned about $3 million from furs, making it one of their best year's recently.

Agriculture

The settlement of rural Manitoba was based mainly on agriculture and agriculture is still a mainstay. In 1995, crops, livestock and direct payments to farmers were worth almost $2.5 billion.

Wheat is still Manitoba's most important crop. It accounts for more than half of total crop production value. Canola and barley are next in importance, followed by flaxseed, oats and rye. Manitoba is one of the world's major producers of flax.

Thanks to fertile soils, adequate precipitation and a few extra days in the growing season, Manitoba's 27 000 farmers have been able to diversify their crops more than farmers in the other prairie provinces. Crops such as buckwheat, sunflower seeds, sugar beets and lentils do well, and there is a thriving vegetable-growing business in south central communities like Altona, Morden and Portage la Prairie.

Most of Manitoba's major livestock production is located in the Interlake region and the southwestern corner of the province. The

The Dauphin railway station. The Dauphin area was first settled in the early 1880s but grew very slowly until the railway arrived in 1896. The town is now a prosperous supply and distribution centre for the region, which includes rich agricultural land and popular tourist areas.

Farming is more diversified in Manitoba than in the other two Prairie Provinces. While it plays a lesser economic role that it once did, it remains important not only to the economy but as a way of life that many are concerned about preserving.

heart of the dairy industry, on the other hand, is located closer to its main market, Winnipeg.

The average size of farms is about 300 hectares (700 acres). In all, about 7.7 million hectares (19 million acres) of Manitoba land is farmed.

To handle Manitoba's grain, there were close to 300 licensed grain elevators in the province. Their total capacity is around 1.4 million tonnes. Manitoba is also a centre for grain marketing, transport and insurance, as well as for the production of agricultural chemicals and fertilizers and the manufacture of farm machinery.

In 1995, Manitoba provided agriculture-related employment for about 40 000 people. They provided supplies and services for farmers and for processing, storing, moving, and selling agricultural products after they leave the farm. In 1990, five of the ten largest companies in Manitoba were involved in the agriculture sector.

Agricultural research is also important in the province. Most of it is carried out at three federal research stations — at Brandon, Morden and on campus at the University of Manitoba in Winnipeg. The Faculty of Agriculture also carries out research and training. Manitoba researchers develop new strains of grains and other plants, look for better ways to manage grain and livestock operations and find improved ways to manage soil fertility and control weeds.

Canada's national grain export marketing corporation, the Canadian Wheat Board, is located in Winnipeg. Just a few blocks away from it is the Winnipeg Commodity Exchange, where Canadian prices for the lower grades of wheat and barley are established, as well as prices for canola, flaxseed and oats.

Manufacturing and Resource Industries

Manufacturing is the largest sector of Manitoba's economy. In 1995, it provided more than 62 000 jobs, and the items produced were valued at just under $8 billion. Some of the leading manufactured products include processed food, transportation equipment, printing and publishing, clothing and textiles, and machinery and metal work.

In Manitoba as in most Canadian provinces, natural resources play an important role in the economy. Mining, energy and forest products are the main components.

Nickel is the leading metal produced from Manitoba mines. It is mined in the Thompson region of northern Manitoba. In recent years, nickel has accounted for about one-third the dollar value of all minerals produced in the province. Copper is the second most important metal. Most of the province's copper is produced in the

Right: Copper and zinc mine at Ruttan Lake.
Lower right: Hydroelectric drilling, Limestone.
Below: Hydroelectric installation on the Nelson River.

Flin Flon region. Other important metals mined in Manitoba include zinc, gold, lead, selenium, tantalum, tellurium and cobalt.

Manitoba is one of the luckiest provinces in terms of its ability to generate hydro–electric energy. In most years, more than 90 percent of all the province's electrical energy comes from water power. Major hydro systems are in place on the Winnipeg and Saskatchewan rivers, but most of the power is generated in the northern half of the province, on the Nelson River system, and transmitted south on special high voltage lines. As of March 31, 1990, the province was capable of generating almost 4 million kilowatts of electrical energy. Surplus power is sold to Saskatchewan, Ontario and the United States.

Far left: **Pouring moulten steel at the Manitoba Rolling Mills, Selkirk.** *Left:* **The government dock at Selkirk.**

Almost all of the petroleum and natural gas produced in Manitoba comes from the southwestern corner of the province, near Virden. In recent years the value of production has been between $100 million and $200 million. Manitoba is home to one of Canada's nuclear research centres, located at Pinawa, on the Winnipeg River, about an hour's drive northeast of Winnipeg.

Forestry is a small but significant factor in Manitoba's economy. In 1992 about 1.6 million cubic metres (2 million cubic yards) of wood were harvested and about $500 million worth of lumber, pulp and paper products were produced. The Pas and Pine Falls are the industry's main centres.

The Service Industries

Services have long been important in Manitoba's economy. Right from the beginning, enterprising Manitobans made fortunes providing transportation, storage, banking, communication and a host of other services.

In recent years, the service industries have provided about three-quarters of the province's gross production. In March 1992 there were 174 000 people employed in the service sector — more than a third of Manitoba's labour force. Four of the province's top ten companies, and six of the ten fastest-growing firms were in the service sector.

CHAPTER 11

Arts and Recreation

The remoteness from any large population centre other than Winnipeg and the richness of the province's ethnic diversity have combined to provide a cultural formula that has encouraged Manitobans to excel in the arts. Over the years, this sparsely populated province has produced some of the nation's most outstanding writers, architects, artists and performers. These include novelist Margaret Laurence, sculptor Leo Mol, artist Jackson Beardy and film maker Kim Johnson.

As Manitoba has grown, so has the diversity of its cultural activities. The province is home to a world-famous ballet company, one of Canada's top theatre groups, a major symphony orchestra, a world class annual folk festival and one of the nation's leading schools of music. The pool of talent from which top performers are drawn is the dozens of orchestras, choirs, drama groups and dance troupes that thrive all across the province.

This banquet of artistic and literary delights does not come at the expense of talent in sports. There's professional hockey, football and soccer, world class curling and horse racing. For those who would rather take part than watch, there are all kinds of amateur sports, from cricket to sailing, from swimming to dog sledding. And for people who simply want to be outdoors, there is an array of riches, whether the preference is for hunting, fishing or just hiking and camping.

The Winnipeg Art Gallery houses contemporary, historical and decorative art as well as the world's largest collection of Inuit art.

The Performing Arts

Every August, hundreds of Manitobans display their talents during Winnipeg's Folklorama festival. For two weeks, people from more than forty ethnic backgrounds proudly display their cultural heritage through drama, dance, song and crafts. And Folklorama is just one of the major cultural attractions during the summer months, a time of year when the performing arts are supposed to take a back seat to other activities.

For four days each July, Bird's Hill Provincial Park just outside of Winnipeg becomes the folk song capital of North America. The Winnipeg Folk Festival has been attracting singers and other musicians from all over the continent for more than twenty years. Another July event is the week-long Fringe Festival, a collection of plays and revues, most of them written in Manitoba. Meanwhile, in a rain-protected amphitheatre in Winnipeg's Kildonan Park, the city's longest-running summer entertainment package plays to large crowds. Rainbow Stage offers two productions of classic broadway musicals each summer.

One of the season's first festivals, the Eckhardt-Grammatté National Music Competition, takes place in May at Brandon University. There's an International Old-Time Fiddle Contest at the International Peace Garden south of Boissevain in western Manitoba in June; the Worldfest Concert of ethnic music in Thompson and the Cripple Creek Music Festival of bluegrass, country and gospel music at Morden in July. August brings the Brandon Folk Music and Art Festival, and in Gimli, on Lake Winnipeg, a rock festival called Sunfest.

The Manitoba Theatre Centre, founded in 1958 by John Hirsch, one of Canada's leading theatre directors, became a model for other regional theatres across the country. It presents half a dozen plays a year on its main stage, and smaller, more experimental productions on its second stage in the nearby Warehouse Theatre. Less well known but just as highly praised is the Cercle Molière, the French-

Left: **The Cercle Molière in a production of Molière's** *Georges Dandin.* *Right:* **The Manitoba Theatre Centre in a production of** *The Magic Trumpet.*

language theatre based in St. Boniface. Established in 1925, it is thought to be the oldest operating French-language theatre group in the country. Other cultural activities in French are presented at the Centre culturel franco-manitobain and at St. Boniface College.

Manitoba's theatre groups are not all old and established. The Prairie Theatre Exchange began in the 1980s. Each season it produces one or more plays that were written locally, as well as other Canadian productions. In 1990 the refurbished Odeon Theatre reverted to its old name, the Walker Theatre, and once again became a venue for stage and musical productions, along with the Playhouse Theatre across from the Centennial Concert Hall.

For those who prefer music and dance, the sixty-seven-piece Winnipeg Symphony Orchestra performs almost every weekend from October until May. Like the Manitoba Theatre Centre, it is nationally recognized, and the Canadian Broadcasting Corporation

Left: **Laura Graham in the Royal Winnipeg Ballet production of** *Ballo Della Regina*. *Right:* **The Crash Test Dummies.**

records its performances regularly. The Winnipeg Chamber Orchestra features many of the same musicians as the Symphony, and like it has a large and loyal following, as does the Manitoba Opera Association.

Popular musicians from Manitoba have achieved national and world success. One of the best known is singer and songwriter Burton Cummings, who grew up in Winnipeg's North End and whose musical group, The Guess Who, rose to the top of the popular song charts between 1968 and 1975. Cummings began a solo career in 1976, and won Juno Awards for Male Vocalist of the Year in 1976 and 1979. One member of the Guess Who, Randy Bachman, split away from the group in 1970 and started Bachman Turner Overdrive. By 1977, BTO had sold 20 million records worldwide. Another Winnipeg rock group, The Crash Test Dummies, took the country by storm in the early nineties.

Other musicians who got their start in Winnipeg include jazz guitarist Lenny Breau, singer-songwriter Neil Young, singer Gisèle MacKenzie and *chansonnier* Daniel Lavoie.

Manitoba's dancers have won world acclaim on several occasions. Two prima ballerinas from the Royal Winnipeg Ballet have won major awards at the International Ballet Competitions at Varna, Bulgaria. Evelyn Hart won a gold meal in 1980, and Laura Graham won a silver in 1989. The Royal Winnipeg Ballet regularly goes on tour to perform in cities all over the world. Winnipeg's Contemporary Dancers have also performed to high praise nationally and abroad.

The best young dancers can study at the Royal Winnipeg Ballet School of Dance, and musicians can follow up with training at one of the two university Schools of Music — one at Brandon University and one at the University of Manitoba. And so it appears that the parade of talent will continue in generations to come.

Art

Walter Phillips studied art against his father's wishes and came to Manitoba from England in 1913, when he was twenty-nine years old. His etchings, woodcuts and prints show his talent as an observer of the land around him. Phillips was one of the few Manitoba artists who was able to make a living exclusively from his work during the 1930s. More recently, the works of Ivan Eyre, Wanda Koop, Don Reichert and Esther Warkov have won acclaim.

The province's architects have been producing award-winning structures for many years. One of the first was John D. Atchison. He brought the newest ideas in architecture to Winnipeg when he arrived from Chicago in 1904. Over the next eighteen years he left his mark on the city, as he designed nearly a hundred buildings.

Since the sixties, the works of Étienne Gaboury have come to dominate the landscape of St. Boniface. Gaboury, who grew up in Swan Lake in southwestern Manitoba has also designed buildings throughout the city as well as in Africa and Mexico. Recently Ron Keenberg of Ikoy has been creating a stir by emphasizing basic structures with strong lines and bold colours.

Above: The Winnipeg Mint, designed by Manitoba architect Etienne Gaboury. *Inset:* Lionel LeMoine FitzGerald's painting *Stooks and Trees. Right:* Inuit sculptor at work.

Literature

Many Manitobans have made outstanding literary contributions. One poet, Sarah Binks, achieved this distinction even though she never existed! Her life and work are all the creation of chemistry professor Paul Hiebert, and they won him the Stephen Leacock Medal for Humour in 1947.

Manitoba writers continue to win awards. Carol Shields won the coveted Pulitzer Prize in 1995 for her novel, *The Stone Diaries*. The University of Manitoba professor was eligible for the American award because she was born in Chicago.

The province's two most famous writers are Margaret Laurence and Gabrielle Roy. Laurence set several of her novels in a small prairie town modelled on her own home-town of Neepawa. One of the best known is *A Jest of God*, which won the Governor General's Award for literature in 1966. Others are *The Diviners*, which won the same award in 1974, and *The Stone Angel*, the first Canadian novel to become required reading for students in France.

Gabrielle Roy's first novel, *Bonheur d'Occasion (The Tin Flute)* was an instant success and won her both the Governor General's Award (her first of three) and the Prix Fémina, one of France's major literary prizes. Several of her later novels were set in St. Boniface, where she grew up, and in the small Manitoba villages where she taught school.

Other Manitoba writers include Sondra Gotlieb, a two-time winner of the Leacock Medal, Adele Wiseman, George Woodstock, David Arnason and Nellie McClung, who was a best-selling novelist before becoming even more famous for her role in winning women the right to vote. Sandra Birdsell won the W.H. Smith Books in Canada First Novel Award for her 1989 book, *The Missing Child*. Birdsell also is known for her short stories and plays.

As well, Canadian writer Ernest Thompson Seton wrote some of his best-known nature stories, including *Wild Animals I have Known*, when he lived in the Carberry area in southwestern Manitoba around the turn of the century. Conservation writer Grey Owl lived for a time during the 1930s in Riding Mountain National Park.

Manitoba has even made a contribution in the publishing of popular literature. Businessman Richard Bonnycastle was the founder of the Harlequin Romance publishing company. That firm was eventually bought by the *Toronto Star*.

Sports

Hockey, ringette and curling in winter, and golf and soccer in summer — those are some of the most popular sporting activities in Manitoba. Each winter thousands of children of all ages take to the hundreds of hockey arenas around the province. It seems there is at least one hockey or ringette league for every age group, including the old-timers!

Over the years Manitoba has produced many National Hockey League (NHL) stars, including Bill Juzda, Bill Mosienko and Terry Sawchuk from Winnipeg, Bobby Clarke from Flin Flon and Reggie Leach from Riverton.

Skating on the duck pond at Winnipeg's Assiniboine Park.

Professionally, the Winnipeg Jets represented Manitoba in the NHL until 1996 when the franchise moved to Phoenix, Arizona. The Jets began as a World Hockey Association (WHA) franchise in 1972. Among NHL players who jumped to the new league was superstar Bobby Hull, who joined the Jets. With Hull, the Jets won three of the seven WHA championships before the league merged with the NHL in 1979. Now the city has a new International Hockey League team known as the Manitoba Moose.

In the weeks leading up to the start of the hockey season, the attention of Manitoba sports fans is focused on the Winnipeg Blue Bombers of the Canadian Football League (CFL). The Bombers were the first Western Canadian team ever to win the Canadian championship Grey Cup in 1935. In the 1950s and 1960s, they won the Grey Cup four times under Bud Grant, who moved on to a successful coaching career with the Minnesota Vikings of the National Football League. More recently, the Bombers won the Grey Cup in 1988 and 1990.

Left: **Randy Carlyle formerly of the Winnipeg Jets; assistant coach for the first season of the Manitoba Moose.** *Right:* **The Winnipeg Blue Bombers.**

Canoeing and windsurfing are popular summer sports in Manitoba. In winter jam-can curling is a favourite with youngsters.

There's another winter game that many Manitobans play with enthusiasm — curling. The Manitoba Curling Association (MCA) Bonspiel, is the world's biggest curling tournament, with as many as 1000 rinks, or teams, taking part.

Some of the best curlers of all time have come from Manitoba — curlers like Don Duguid, Billy Walsh, Howard "Pappy" Wood, and a high school kid named Terry Braunstein, who almost won the Canadian championship in 1959. Perhaps the best curler of them all was Ken Watson of Minnedosa. Watson was the first to win the national championship three times, and he won six grand aggregate trophies in a row in the MCA bonspiel — from 1942 to 1947 — a record that has never been matched. His book *Ken Watson on Curling* sold nearly 150 000 copies and is considered by many to be *the* book on the subject.

With its thousands of lakes and rivers, Manitoba is a paradise for fishermen, young and old.

Other professional sports available in Winnipeg are baseball, basketball and horseracing.

Throughout the province there are all kinds of amateur facilities — for swimming, tennis, track, baseball, volleyball, lacrosse and golf, to name a few. Two golfers — Dan Halldorson of Brandon and George Knudson of Winnipeg — have had successful careers on the U.S. professional golf circuit. One year Knudson came within one stroke of winning the Master's tournament in Augusta, Georgia.

For those who prefer less competitive outdoor activities, there is camping, backpacking and hiking throughout the province. Fishermen looking for a special angling thrill can find outfitters who will fly them to remote lakes where the fish are as large and as plentiful as they were before the Europeans arrived in North America.

CHAPTER 12

A Tour of Manitoba

Manitoba's diversity is reflected in the range of activities there are for residents and visitors to do in the province.

There's an amazing variety of museums, parks and historical sites. Summer and winter, there are stage productions, concerts, dance programs, fairs and festivals. There's swimming and skiing, canoeing and viewing — something for every season and for every taste in Manitoba!

Winnipeg

The biggest collection of cultural and sightseeing activities is to be found in Winnipeg. A visitor can browse through the shops at the Forks, examine the paintings and sculpture at the Winnipeg Art Gallery, visit one of Canada's major zoos or walk through a tropical garden in mid-winter.

There are no fewer than thirty museums to pick from in and around Winnipeg. The best-known is the Manitoba Museum of Man and Nature, with its mix of historic and natural settings. One of the favorite displays is the replica of the *Nonsuch*, the ship that carried the first Hudson's Bay Company traders to Manitoba. It is considered the most accurate reproduction ever made of a seventeenth-century ship, and the best thing about it is that visitors are welcome to climb aboard.

Beside the museum is a planetarium, which offers a variety of programs on the wonders of the universe. Across the street is the

Fall's displays of colour tend to be less spectacular in Manitoba than in eastern Canada, but they have their own beauty. *Inset:* Polar bear at the Winnipeg zoo.

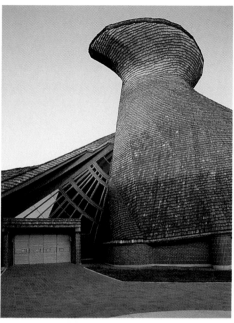

Left: The facade of the St. Boniface Basilica survived a 1968 fire and was incorporated into the design of the new church. *Right:* A few blocks away the dramatic Precious Blood Church, designed by Etienne Gaboury, stands in striking contrast to traditional church architecture as exemplified by the basilica facade.

Winnipeg City Hall, and a couple of blocks away is the Exchange District — one of Canada's best collections of heritage architecture.

Other popular museums include the house once owned by Sir Hugh John Macdonald, son of the first prime minister and, for a brief time, premier of Manitoba; the Manitoba Children's Museum, western Canada's first hands-on museum designed specifically for children; and the Ukrainian Museum, located in the Holy Trinity Ukrainian Orthodox Cathedral.

Holy Trinity is just one of Winnipeg's interesting churches. Many others are worth a visit, especially the St. Boniface Basilica, across the Red River in St. Boniface. Métis leader Louis Riel is buried in the churchyard. Nearby is a museum that used to be the home of the Grey Nuns.

Other places of interest include Lower Fort Garry, located just north of the city, which offers re-enactments of life at the fort dur-

Left: The restored fur loft at Lower Fort Garry National Historic Park. *Above left:* This replica of the 17th-century ship *Nonsuch* is one of the Museum of Man and Nature's most popular exhibits. *Above right:* Cycling on one of Winnipeg's pleasant residential streets.

ing the 1800s. And there are regular tours of the Manitoba Legislature and its magnificent grounds and of the Winnipeg Mint, where most of Canada's coins are made.

When tired of sightseeing, summer visitors can enjoy a stroll along the pleasant tree-lined streets of the city's residential districts or relax amid the flower gardens and lawns of one of its many small and large parks. Or they can take a two-hour ride aboard the Prairie Dog Central, a vintage steam-driven train, or a river-boat cruise on the Red River.

The midway at Winnipeg's Red River Exhibition, held each year in late June.
Inset: A guaranteed cure for mid-winter blues is St. Boniface's Festival du
Voyageur, which features ice-sculpture displays, fiddling and jigging contests and
a variety of other indoor and outdoor activities and entertainments.

Rural Manitoba

Directly north of Winnipeg is Lake Winnipeg. On the east shore, at
Grand Beach and Victoria Beach, is some of the finest lakeside sand
anywhere on earth. On the lake's west shore are more beaches and
the fishing and farming town of Gimli, home of the annual Icelandic Festival.

East of Winnipeg lies the province's biggest provincial park, the
Whiteshell. Among the park's two hundred lakes is the province's
deepest, West Hawk Lake, and one called Lily Pond that is over-
looked by cliffs made up of rock that is more than three billion
years old. Travellers who veer south of the main highway on the
way to the Whiteshell can stop in at Steinbach, where they can visit
a restored Mennonite pioneer village.

Restored buildings at the Mennonite Heritage Village include dwellings, a blacksmith shop, a schoolhouse and a working wind-powered grist mill.

South of Winnipeg, about halfway to the U.S. border, is the town of Morris. The Morris Stampede, which takes place every July, is the second-largest rodeo in the country, after the world famous Calgary Stampede. Southwest of Morris is Morden, home of the annual Corn and Apple Festival, and the site of one of the three main agricultural research stations in the province.

One of the trading posts from the fur trading days was Fort la Reine, near what is now the city of Portage la Prairie. That city, about forty-five minutes' drive west of Winnipeg, has built a replica of old Fort la Reine just outside of town. Still farther west, on the

Top: **The Morris Stampede.** *Above:* **The Austin Threshermen's Reunion.** *Right:* **Boissevain's Tommy the Turtle identifies the town as the home of Canada's only international turtle-racing competition.** *Far right:* **Petroforms — boulders laid out by natives centuries ago in the shape of fish, reptiles and birds — near Betula Lake in the Whiteshell.**

Trans-Canada Highway, is the town of Austin. There, every August, farmers get out their vintage harvesting equipment — binders, tractors and an old threshing machine — as they celebrate the Threshermen's Reunion.

About halfway between the Trans-Canada Highway and Highway 2, which also runs east and west, is Manitoba's desert. It's not very big, but it's real, with sand dunes and cacti.

A little further on, about 200 kilometres (124 miles) west of Winnipeg, is the province's second largest city, Brandon. Brandon

The International Peace garden on the Manitoba–North Dakota border is dedicated to continuing peace between Canada and the United States.

features a university, a pleasant location on the banks of the Assiniboine River and easy access to many lakes and parks. It also hosts two major provincial fairs — the Provincial Exhibition and the Royal Manitoba Winter Fair.

To the south of Brandon, on the Manitoba-North Dakota border, is one of the prettiest gardens in the province. It's the International Peace Garden. Located half on the American side and half on the Canadian side of the border, it symbolizes the good relationship enjoyed between Canada and the United States.

To the southwest of Brandon is the town of Souris, of special interest to rock collectors because there are interesting gemstones in the area.

Riding Mountain National Park is directly north of Brandon. Almost 3000 square kilometres (1160 square miles) in area, it has several lakes and many riding and hiking trails, and is located beside Mount Agassiz, one of Manitoba's best ski hills. More parkland and the Duck and Porcupine mountains stretch northwestward to the Saskatchewan border.

The northern mining towns of Thompson and Flin Flon offer some of the best sport fishing anywhere in the world. Those prepared to go even farther north to Churchill, on the Hudson Bay coast, can watch beluga whales frolicking in the bay. But Churchill is most famous as a place to watch polar bears, especially in the fall, as they wait for the Churchill River to freeze before migrating into the Northwest Territories. In 1996, *Wapusk* (Cree for white bear) *National Park* was established southeast of Churchill. With 11 475 km (4,431 sq. mi.), it is Canada's seventh largest national park.

The most dramatic scenery is farthest away, in the northern half of the province. There the highways are most often rivers meandering through the rocks and forest. Sometimes they are funnelled through rocky channels where canoeists must portage around the white water rapids; other times they widen into lakes.

But there is also a special beauty in and around the small communities that dot southern Manitoba. Many, like La Rivière, are not far from the United States border. Located among the gently rolling hills on the Pembina River, it defies the prairie flatland stereotype. So do Souris in the southwest, with its swinging bridge across the

In summer, white beluga whales surface and dive in the greeenish blue waters at the mouth of the Churchill River.

Sun dogs — a phenomenon caused by the reflection of the sun's rays off the vertical face of ice-cystals in the air.

Souris River, Minnedosa, to the south of Riding Mountain National Park, and any number of other towns and villages.

Along the Trans-Canada Highway you will find the classic prairie landscape — fields of grain that stretch as far as the eye can see, punctuated by the silhouette of a prairie grain elevator. There is variety and a special beauty even here, that changes with the season, the time of day, and the way the sky and clouds present the light.

Manitoba's beauty is unassuming, but the landscape is only a part of it. Often it is created or enhanced by an azure sky or spectacular cloud formations and the ever-changing variety of prairie sunlight. The purple haze of a midwinter afternoon is a stark contrast to the luxuriant greens of June, the orange afterglow when the sun goes down in August, the spectacle of a summer thunderstorm or a winter display of northern lights, the blaze of colours in early October.

You can confirm the spectacular effects of prairie light by thumbing through any anthology of Manitoba photographs. Better still is to be in Manitoba and see it for yourself.

Top: **Hudson Bay in winter.**
Bottom: **Wheat field near Brandon.**

Facts at a Glance

General Information:

Provincehood: Joined Confederation July 15, 1870

Origin of Name: Probably from the Cree language, referring to the echoing sounds that came from a strait of Lake Manitoba and that were thought to be the voice of the Great Spirit, or Manitou.

Provincial Capital: Winnipeg

Provincial Nickname: Keystone Province

Provincial Flag: The flag is a Red Ensign, with the Union Jack in the upper quarter on the staff side and the provincial coat-of-arms centred in the fly half.

Provincial Bird: Great Gray Owl

Provincial Flower: Prairie Crocus

Population

Population: 1 091 942 (1991 census)

Population Density: 1.68 people per square kilometre (4.35 per sq. mi.) (1991 census)

Population Distribution: 75 percent of Manitobans live in a city or town and 75 percent of those urban dwellers live in Winnipeg.

Winnipeg	652 354
Brandon	38 567
Thompson	14 977
Portage la Prairie	13 186
Flin Flon	7 119

(Population figures based on the 1991 census)

Population Growth: After a population boom in its early years of provincehood, Manitoba has experienced steady growth.

Year	Population
1871	25 228
1891	152 506
1911	461 394
1931	700 139
1951	766 541
1961	921 686
1971	988 000
1981	1 026 241
1986	1 071 232
1991	1 091 942

Geography

Borders: Manitoba is bordered by the American states of Minnesota and North Dakota on the south, Saskatchewan on the west, the Northwest Territories on the north, and Ontario on the east. To the northeast the province has 645 km (400 mi.) of coastline along Hudson Bay.

Highest Point: Baldy Mountain, in Duck Mountain Provincial Park, 831 m (2726 ft.)

Lowest Point: sea level, along the Hudson Bay coast

Greatest Distance:
North to South   1225 km (761 mi.)
East to West   793 km (493 mi.)

Area:
Land surface   548 355 km² (211 665 sq. mi.)
Water Surface   101 592 km² (39 215 sq. mi.)
Total   649 947 km² (250 880 sq. mi.)

Rank in area among provinces: 5th

Time zone: All of Manitoba is located in the Central time zone. Daylight Saving Time is in effect in the province from the first weekend in April to the last weekend in October.

National Forests and Parklands: *Riding Mountain National Park* contains 2987 km² (1150 sq. mi.) of rolling woodland, lakes and streams. Beside Clear Lake is the resort town of Wasagaming, and there is a network of 425 km (264 mi.) of hiking and riding trails. In winter there is downhill skiing at Mount Agassiz, on the eastern slopes of Riding Mountain. In 1991 the courts determined that part of the national park actually belongs to the Kee See Kow Anin Indian band. The band is considering whether to occupy the land or negotiate an agreement that will leave it as part of the park.

Three National Historic Parks preserve and illustrate important aspects of Manitoba's history. The best known is *Lower Fort Garry*, northeast of Winnipeg on the Red River. It has been restored to depict fur trade and Red River Settlement conditions of the mid-19th century. *The Forks*, at the junction of the Red and Assiniboine rivers, was established in 1990 to celebrate the meeting and trading place it has been for many centuries. One of its many attractions is an archaeological dig in which the general public is invited to take part. *Fort Prince of Wales* is located on the coast of Hudson Bay at the mouth of the Churchill River. It is a partially-restored 18th-century stone fort that for centuries was one of the main centres of the fur trade.

There are also three National Historic Sites. *Riel House*, in Winnipeg, was the home of the Riel family (though not of Louis Riel) from 1881 to 1968. It has been restored and furnished as a mid-1880s residence. *St. Andrew's Rectory*, on the Red River, commemorates the role of the early Anglican missionaries in Red River. *York Factory* is located on Hudson

Bay, 240 km (149 mi) southeast of Churchill. Accessible only by chartered aircraft or canoe, it recalls the days of the fur trade and of French-British rivalry for possession of Canada's western interior.

Rivers: All of Manitoba's waters eventually drain into Hudson Bay. The *Nelson*, *Churchill* and *Hayes* rivers, flow directly into Hudson Bay. The *Saskatchewan River* flows into Lake Winnipeg from the west, the *Winnipeg River* from the east, and the *Red River* from the south. Another major river, the *Assiniboine*, joins the Red River at the Forks in Winnipeg.

Lakes: There are tens of thousands of lakes in Manitoba, covering about 15 percent of the province's total area. While most are in the northern three-fifths of the province, the three largest lakes — *Lake Winnipeg*, *Lake Winnipegosis* and *Lake Manitoba* — are in the southern two-fifths. Other major lakes are *God's Lake*, *Southern Indian Lake*, and *Tadoule Lake*.

Topography: Manitoba is the easternmost of the three Prairie Provinces. Parts of southern Manitoba are very flat with rolling hills and valleys dominating the rest. The land slopes gradually from the south and west to sea level in the northeast. In most of the province elevations range between 150 and 300 m (492 and 984 ft.). The land most suitable for agriculture, where most of the people live, lies south and west of Lake Winnipegosis and Lake Winnipeg. The rest is in rugged Precambrian Shield country, and consists mainly of rocks, lakes, rivers and swamps.

Climate: Manitoba has warm, sunny summers and cold, sunny winters. Afternoon temperatures in July and August average 25° C (77° F) in Winnipeg, but mid-winter daytime readings almost always remain well below freezing. Mean January temperatures in Brandon are -19.7° C (-3.6° F) and the monthly mean for July is 18.8° C (65.8° F). At The Pas, January averages -22.7° C (-9° F) and July 17.7° C (64° F). At Churchill the mean for January is -27.5° C (-17.5° f), and for July 11.8° C (53° F).

In Winnipeg, there are normally 121.2 hours of bright sunshine in January, and 315.6 hours in July. Even the cloudiest month, November, averages 90.7 hours of sunshine.

More than half of the annual precipitation falls in the summer months, often in the form of brief but heavy showers. Total average annual precipitation ranges from 355 mm (14 in.) in the far north to 558 mm (22 in.) in the southeast; most agricultural areas receive between 400 and 500 mm (16-20 in.) each year.

Nature

Trees: Aspen, balsam poplar, bur oak, American elm, green ash, Manitoba maple, cottonwood, jack pine, white spruce, black spruce, balsam fir, birch, tamarack, alder

Wild plants: various kinds of willow, grasses, sedges, reeds, mosses, ferns and lichens; wildflowers, including prairie lily, prairie crocus, wild rose, lily of the valley, marsh marigold; wild berries including saskatoon, blueberry, red raspberry, currant, gooseberry

Animals: mammals include bat, rabbit, hare, numerous rodents, beluga whale, coyote, wolf, fox, black bear, polar bear, racoon, several members of the weasel family, cougar, lynx, bobcat, walrus, harbour seal, elk, deer, moose, caribou, pronghorn, bison, muskox; reptiles include turtles, northern prairie skink, and 5 species of snake; there are 13 species of amphibians (salamanders, toads and frogs)

Birds: among the hundreds of bird species that can be seen in Manitoba are loon, pelican, heron, swan, Canada goose, several ducks, bald and golden eagles, hawks, peregrine falcon, partridge, ring-necked pheasant, grouse, sandhill crane, sandpiper, great gray owl, snowy owl, ruby-throated hummingbird, woodpeckers, horned lark, swallows, jays, black-billed magpie, American crow, common raven, black-capped chickadee, bluebird, scarlet tanager, sparrows, bobolink, red-winged blackbird, western meadowlark

Fish: lake sturgeon, lake whitefish,

White poplars.

rainbow trout, brook trout, Arctic grayling, goldeye, mooneye, northern pike, muskellunge, carp, longnose sucker, bullhead, channel catfish, trout-perch, brook stickleback, white bass, smallmouth bass, largemouth bass, yellow perch, yellow walleye, sauger, Arctic char

Wildlife management areas, covering more than 30 000 km² (11 500 sq. mi.), are provided to improve habitat and allow access for people to enjoy wildlife.

Government and the Courts

Governments: Manitoba has 14 seats in the federal House of

104

Commons and 6 seats in the Senate. Provincial laws are passed by a single-chamber Legislative Assembly of 57 members. The premier and his cabinet are sitting members from the party with the most elected members of the legislative assembly.

At the local level municipalities of various kinds are responsible for government services. The province has 5 incorporated cities, 35 incorporated towns, 39 incorporated villages and 105 rural municipalities. The business of municipalities is directed by locally elected councils, subject to some provincial control. Seventeen local government districts (LGDs) administer settled areas that are not incorporated municipalities. The Department of Northern Affairs has jurisdiction in the areas of northern Manitoba not incorporated or organized as LGDs.

Manitobans must be 18 years of age to vote.

The Courts: The Manitoba Court of Appeal is the highest court in the province. It has a chief justice and six other judges, all appointed by the federal government.

The Court of Queen's Bench is the highest trial court. It has a chief justice, an associate chief justice, and several other judges. All are federally appointed. This court rules on civil issues and most criminal cases. It also hears appeals on certain issues referred from Provincial Court. All family and child protection cases heard in Winnipeg and Selkirk come under the family divi-sion of the Court of Queen's Bench, which also runs a Small Claims Court.

Provincial Court deals with minor criminal and civil cases. It also deals with family matters in many parts of the province, and with cases involving persons under the age of 18.

Education

Public school education in Manitoba is administered through 47 school divisions and 10 school districts. Enrolment in public schools in the 1992-93 school year was almost 200 000 and about 15 000 teachers were employed in the system. Elementary and secondary education is offered through 12 grades. The language of instruction is usually English or French, but the Heritage Language Program makes it possible to present school curriculum in other languages. Thirty schools offer vocational-industrial programs. Four schools offer co-operative vocational-industrial education, and almost every high school offers business education programs.

The province supports three community colleges — Assiniboine in Brandon, Keewatin in The Pas and Red River in Winnipeg. These colleges offer a variety of programs on a full-time or part-time basis at the colleges' main campuses, at several regional centres and in more than 120 communities. During 1989-90, nearly 30 000 students were enrolled in full-time community college courses.

Manitoba has three universities —
the University of Manitoba, the University of Winnipeg and Brandon
University.

The University of Manitoba is on
a 276-ha (685-acre) campus. It has
about 14 400 full-time, 8200 part-time
and 6800 summer students. There are
four affiliated colleges — St. John's,
St. Paul's, St. Andrew's and University College. In addition, St. Boniface
College, located off campus in St.
Boniface, offers instruction in
French, and the health sciences
faculties are located near the Health
Sciences Centre.

The University of Winnipeg has
about 2700 full-time, 4500 part-time
and 2800 summer students. Located
in downtown Winnipeg, it offers
undergraduate degrees in Arts, Science, Education, Theology, and a
limited number of graduate programs.

Brandon University offers undergraduate degrees in Arts, Science,
Education and Music, and a master's
degree in Music. It has about 1200
full-time, 1600 part-time and 1400
summer students.

Economy and Industry

Manitoba has a highly diversified
economy. Resources, manufacturing
and services each make an important
contribution. In 1995, Manitoba's
Gross Domestic Product was more
than $26 billion at market prices.
Public and private investment
totalled almost $4 billion.

Primary Products:

Agriculture: Wheat continues to
be the most important Manitoba
crop, accounting for over half of crop
production value. It is followed by
barley, canola, flaxseed, oats and
rye. Specialized crops such as sunflowers, buckwheat, corn, soybeans,
lentils and field peas are also important as are horticulture and livestock.
In 1995, farm cash receipts totalled
almost $2.5 billion.

Minerals: In 1995, Manitoba's mineral production was valued at just
over $1 billion. Metals accounted for
more than 80 percent of the total
value, followed by industrial
minerals and petroleum. Nickel
production is the most important
component, followed by copper.

Industrial minerals quarried in
Manitoba include a wide variety of
raw materials for construction and
specialized uses. Portland cement is
produced at Fort Whyte, near
Winnipeg, using local sand and
limestone quarried near Steep Rock.
Limestone is also quarried north of
Mafeking. Lime is produced at
Faulkner. Dolomitic limestone is
quarried at Garson for Tyndall
building stone, and granite near
Pinawa and Whitemouth. High-
quality silica sand quarried on Black
Island in Lake Winnipeg has several
uses, including glass-making.

Much of Manitoba's resource and
manufacturing output is exported. In
1995, the province's exports were
worth well over $5 billion. About
$4 billion of this amount went to the
United States.

Minnedosa, in southwestern Manitoba, is considered one of Manitoba's prettiest towns.

Energy: Manitoba is a net exporter of hydro-electric power. Its Crown corporation, Manitoba Hydro, has an installed capacity of 4 million kilowatts and there is potential capacity for another 6 million kilowatts. Most of the generating stations are north of the 53rd parallel, on the Nelson, Saskatchewan and Laurie rivers. In 1989, the province's petroleum production was valued at $91.8 million.

Fishing: Even though Manitoba is almost landlocked, there is a significant freshwater fishing industry. In 1988-89, Manitoba's fisheries were worth about $23.5 million. The largest three lakes produce about 70 percent of the total catch of about 13 million kg (28 million lb.) Whitefish, pike, walleye and sauger are the most important of the 14 species that are commercially caught.

Forestry: Over half of Manitoba's total area is officially classified as forest land — more than triple the amount dedicated to agriculture. Fifteen areas, with a total of 21 900 km^2 (8450 sq. mi.) are set aside as publicly owned provincial forests, specifically for producing forest products. The

forest industry has total sales of close to $500 million, much of it to markets outside Manitoba. More than 90 percent of the wood harvested is used for pulpwood and sawlogs.

Manufacturing: In 1995, establishments engaged in manufacturing employed about 52 000 people and accounted for about 10 percent of provincial employment. Their total production was worth just under $8 billion.

The most important industries are food and beverages, machinery, primary metal and metal fabricating, transportation equipment and clothing, which account for about two-thirds of the total. An estimated 48 percent of output is exported to other parts of Canada, and a further 10 percent is sent abroad.

Services:

Transportation: Manitoba maintains a 500-km (300-mile) stretch of the Trans-Canada Highway from Ontario to Saskatchewan as well as a section of the Yellowhead Route, which proceeds northwest from Portage la Prairie to the Saskatchewan border on its way to Edmonton. North-south highways include the 800-km (500-mile) route from the United States border at Turtle Mountain to Flin Flon and the highway linking Winnipeg and Thompson through the Interlake region. As of April 1, 1989 there were more than 7000 km (4300 mi.) of provincial trunk highways in Manitoba and 12 000 km (7500 mi.) of provincial roads.

Railways haul a large proportion of freight moving to, from, and within Manitoba. Canadian National has 4100 km (2500 mi.) of main track in Manitoba. CN's Symington Yards is one of the most modern rail marshalling yards of its kind. The railway's Transcona shops in Winnipeg are CN's western Canadian base for all major repairs to locomotives and rail cars. CN also maintains a national training centre at Gimli. Canadian Pacific has 2500 km (1500 mi.) of mainline track and over 800 km (500 mi.) of sidings and yard track in Manitoba. Its marshalling yard processes an average of 2000 freight cars each day. Its Weston shops are one of three heavy repair facilities in the CP Rail system.

Air services: Air Canada operates frequent passenger and cargo flights from Winnipeg to domestic points east and west, and to some American points. Canadian Airlines International also has frequent domestic flights. Northwest Orient Airlines of Minneapolis operates daily flights to the American midwest and Florida. Smaller airlines include Perimeter Airlines, Northland-Air Manitoba and Calm Air. There are 104 licensed commercial air carriers in Manitoba. They operate a variety of services, such as flight training, aerial photography, and surveying, crop dusting, and passenger and freight service to many Manitoba points.

Although Manitoba is a central plains province, it also has one Maritime port — at Churchill, on Hudson Bay. It offers a short route to European markets, since it is only 4725 km (3000 mi.) from Liverpool England. The port handles about 500 000 tonnes of grain in most years, as well as bulk cargo and fuel oil. Hudson Bay and Hudson Strait are normally navigable from mid-July to mid-November.

Communications: The Manitoba Telephone System, owned by the provincial government and directed by a board of commissioners, operates a wide range of sophisticated telecommunications services throughout the province.

There are several AM and FM stations in Winnipeg, and others are located in Altona, Boissevain, Brandon, Cross Lake, Norway House, Dauphin, Flin Flon, Portage la Prairie, Selkirk, Steinbach, The Pas, Thompson and Winkler. The Canadian Broadcasting Corporation has English- and French-language rebroadcasters at points throughout rural Manitoba.

There are television stations in Brandon, Portage la Prairie and Thompson, as well as four in Winnipeg, including a French-language CBC-TV station. All have rebroadcasters in various parts of the province.

Manitoba has six daily newspapers. In addition, one paper publishes twice a week, one publishes three times a week, and there are about 60 weeklies, most of which are community newspapers and some of which are ethnic publications. There are also a number of small book publishers in Manitoba.

Social and Cultural Life

Museums: There are about 130 museums in Manitoba, 30 of which are in Winnipeg. There are museums commemorating, among other things, native history and the fur trade, pioneer heritage, history, science, sports, aviation, agriculture and farm implements, shipping, clothing, mining and automobiles. The biggest is the Manitoba Museum of Man and Nature, a natural history and pioneer museum, and its companion, the Planetarium. Other museums include those at Upper and Lower Fort Garry, the St. Boniface Museum, the Living Prairie Museum in west Winnipeg, the Western Canada Aviation Museum, the Mennonite Heritage Museum in Steinbach, the B.J. Hales Museum of Natural History in Brandon, the Dugald Costume Museum in Dugald, the Fort la Reine Museum at Portage la Prairie and the Lynn Lake Mining Town Museum.

Manitoba has western Canada's finest collection of heritage buildings, many of which are still in use.

Festivals: Manitoba has more than 50 festivals that reflect the richness of its resources and the cultural backgrounds of its people. Outstanding among them are the Provincial Exhibition of Manitoba in Brandon, Folklorama in Winnipeg, the Icelandic Festival in Gimli, the Winnipeg Folk Festival, Canada's National Ukrainian Festival in Dauphin, Opasquia Indian days in The Pas, Pioneer Days in Steinbach, York Boat Days in Nor-

way House, Thompson Nickel Days in Thompson, Frog Follies in St. Pierre, the Manitoba Stampede in Morris, the Trout Festival in Flin Flon, the Fête Franco-Manitobaine in La Broquerie, the Threshermen's Reunion in Austin and the Corn and Apple Festival in Morden. Winter festivals include the Festival du Voyageur in Winnipeg, the Trappers' Festival in The Pas, the Canadian Power Toboggan Championships in Beausejour and the Royal Manitoba Winter Fair in Brandon.

Performing Arts: The Manitoba Theatre Centre is a nationally recognized institution. In addition, Winnipeg residents can see productions at the Warehouse Theatre, the Prairie Theatre Exchange, Le Cercle Molière and several small production houses, and attend performances of the internationally acclaimed Royal Winnipeg Ballet, Winnipeg's Contemporary Dancers, the Winnipeg Symphony Orchestra, the Manitoba Opera Association and the Winnipeg Chamber Orchestra.

Sports and Recreation: Manitobans can watch International Hockey League action with the Manitoba Moose, football with the Winnipeg Blue Bombers of the CFL, baseball with the Winnipeg Goldeyes of the Northern League or basketball with the Winnipeg Cyclone of the International Basketball Association. There is also plenty of minor hockey action with Western Hockey league teams in Brandon (the Wheat Kings) and Flin Flon (the Bombers), as well as the Manitoba Junior Hockey League and university hockey. The three universities also take part in intercollegiate basketball, volleyball and various other sports.

Manitoba has more than 15 000 km² (5800 sq. mi.) of provincial parks. The system comprises a wilderness park, 8 natural parks, 42 recreation parks, 61 wayside parks, 8 heritage parks and one special-use park. There are parks designated for picnicking, swimming, canoeing, hunting, fishing, golfing, horseback riding, as well as downhill and cross-country skiing, snowshoeing, tobogganing and snowmobiling.

Historic Sites and Landmarks

Canada's National Ukrainian Festival, Inc., Dauphin, displays a collection of Ukrainian pioneer artifacts, embroidery, Easter eggs, and other handicrafts.

Dugald Costume Museum and Pioneer Home, Dugald, has a 13 000-piece costume collection that dates from 1765, inside a fully restored pioneer home built about 1886.

Eskimo Museum, in Churchill, has a collection of Inuit carvings and artifacts that date from Pre-Dorset (1700 B.C.) to modern times.

The Forks National Historic Site, at the junction of the Red and Assiniboine rivers, offers a variety of displays and activities.

Fort Dauphin Museum, Dauphin, is a replica of a North West Company fur trade fort. It includes a trapper's cabin, pioneer house, blacksmith shop, store, school house, church and an archaeological laboratory.

Fort la Reine Museum, Portage la Prairie, features a village showing native and pioneer artifacts depicting life from the early 1700s.

Grant's Old Mill, Winnipeg, is a replica of the original watermill built on Sturgeon Creek in 1829 by the family of Métis leader Cuthbert Grant. Grist is ground each day there during summer and sold in souvenir bags.

Hecla Village was settled in 1876 by Icelanders. Vestiges of the original fishing village still remain on the east side of Hecla Island, on Lake Winnipeg, and are being restored.

Lower Fort Garry National Historic Park is a restoration of a fort that was first built in the 1830s as a provisioning and supply centre for the Hudson's Bay Company.

Manitoba Agricultural Hall of Fame, in the Agricultural Extension Centre, in Brandon, showcases persons who have made outstanding contributions to agriculture or rural living.

Manitoba Agricultural Museum, Austin, is located on a 20-ha (50-acre) site that depicts a pioneer village with machines, tools and household effects. The annual Threshermen's Reunion, is held here in late July.

Manitoba Museum of Man and Nature, Winnipeg, features natural history and geological history displays, as well as an important display of pioneer Winnipeg. The *Planetarium* is located beside the museum.

Margaret Laurence House, Neepawa, contains two tribute rooms devoted to the author. There are autographed books, personal possessions, memorabilia and photographs.

Mennonite Heritage Village, Steinbach, is a pioneer village complex, that includes Canada's only operating wind-powered gristmill.

Morden District Museum houses the largest collection of dinosaur bones in the province.

Pembina Threshermen's Museum, Winkler, features steam threshing equipment in working order, along with other agricultural and pioneer antiques and artifacts.

Prairie Dog Central Steam Train offers a 60-kilometre (37-mile) turn-of-the-century steam train excursion from Winnipeg to Grosse Isle.

Riel House, National Historic Park, Winnipeg, shows the cultural, social and economic aspects of life around St. Boniface in the 1880s.

Seven Oaks House, Winnipeg, is the oldest inhabitable house in Manitoba. John Inkster built it in 1851.

St. Andrew's Church (on-the-Red), and *St. Andrew's Rectory National Historic Park*, north of Winnipeg. The stone church is the oldest Anglican church west of the Great lakes that is still in continuous use; the restored rectory was built in 1850-55.

St. Boniface Basilica, the oldest church in western Canada, was built in 1818 and replaced several times after fires. After the most recent fire in 1968, the facade and walls of the old structure were used in the new design. Louis Riel is buried in the churchyard.

St. Boniface Museum is the oldest building in the City of Winnipeg. Built in 1846, it displays the life of the Métis and the *Canadien* on the prairies.

Western Canada Aviation Museum at the International Airport displays vintage aircraft and related artifacts.

Showing calves at the Shoal Lake Fair.

111

Other Interesting Places to Visit

Assiniboine Park is Winnipeg's oldest park. It includes the Winnipeg Zoo and a conservatory featuring year-round flowers and tropical plants in an indoor setting.

Clearwater Provincial Forestry Nursery, 32 km (20 mi.) northeast of The Pas. Jackpine and black and white spruce trees are raised for provincial reforestation programs.

Delta Marsh, northeast of Portage la Prairie, is one of North America's largest waterfowl staging marshes.

Fort Whyte Centre for Environmental Education is an 80-ha (200-acre) site with prairie habitat, marshes, lakes and bush, as well as plenty of displays and self-guided trails.

Freshwater Institute at the University of Manitoba is a national centre for research in marine life and the ecology of lakes.

International Peace Garden is shared by Manitoba and North Dakota just off Highway 10 south of Boissevain.

Narcisse Wildlife Management Area in the Interlake region features thousands of red-sided garter snakes that emerge from hibernation each spring in late April or early May .

Oak Hammock Marsh, northwest of Winnipeg near Lake Manitoba, is a reclaimed wetland that now is home to more than 260 kinds of birds and 25 mammals.

Oak Lake Goose Refuge, west of Brandon. Geese, ducks, swans, cranes and other wildlife gather here in great numbers each year.

Provincial Legislature, near downtown Winnipeg. It is built from Manitoba tyndall limestone and has been designated a provincial heritage site. Perched atop it is the Golden Boy, a 4-m (13-ft.) statue sheathed in 23.5-karat gold.

Souris Agate Pit has one of the largest varieties of semi-precious stones in North America, including agate, jasper, epidote, petrified wood and dendrite.

Spirit Sands, a tract of sand dunes and rolling hills, is located between the villages of Glenboro and Carberry, in western Manitoba.

Souris, southwest of Brandon, has Canada's longest free suspension bridge spanning the Souris River.

Waterhen Band Wood Bison Project, near Ste. Rose du Lac, is an enclosure 14.5 km^2 (5.6 sq. mi.) in area where a wild herd of wood bison has been established.

Winnipeg Art Gallery, located in downtown Winnipeg. It holds the world's largest collection of Inuit art, as well as contemporary, historical and decorative works.

Winnipeg Commodity Exchange is the largest agricultural exchange in Canada.

Important Dates

Golden Boy, the distinctive statue that stands atop the Legislative Building in Winnipeg.

1612 Sir Thomas Button of England, the first European in present-day Manitoba, explores the west coast of Hudson Bay and spends the winter there.

1670 King Charles II of England issues a charter to the Hudson's Bay Company, giving it authority over the watersheds of all rivers flowing into Hudson Bay.

1682 The Hudson's Bay Company builds York Fort (later known as York Factory) at the mouth of the Hayes River.

1683 French and English traders begin a long series of skirmishes over the Hudson Bay trading posts.

1688 The first Fort Prince of Wales is built at Churchill Harbour.

1690-1692 Henry Kelsey of the Hudson's Bay Company explores inland from Hudson Bay.

1738 La Vérendrye, a French-Canadian fur trader, arrives at the junction of the Red and Assiniboine rivers via the St. Lawrence-Great Lakes route.

1763 Britain gains possession of all French colonies in what is now Canada.

1784 The North West Company is organized by Montreal merchants to compete with the Hudson's Bay Company.

1801 The Métis build the first Red River cart at Fort Pembina.

1811 The first group of Selkirk settlers arrive at York Factory in September.

1816 In a skirmish with the Métis at Seven Oaks, Robert Semple and 20 settlers are killed.

1817 The first treaty is concluded between Europeans and the Indians of the West. Under the treaty, the Swampy Cree and Saulteaux cede land in return for an annual payment.

1818 Britain and the United States fix the Canada-U.S. border at the 49th parallel from the Lake of the Woods to the Rocky Mountains.

1819 St. Boniface College is founded.

1821 The Hudson's Bay Company and the North West Company merge.

1826 The greatest flood in the recorded history of the Red River takes place in May.

1859	Steamboat service begins on the Red River.
1867	The British North America Act is proclaimed creating the Dominion of Canada.
1869-1870	The Métis of Red River resist union with Canada and set up a provisional government under Louis Riel.
1870	The Manitoba Act is passed creating the Province of Manitoba, which is, however, much smaller than today's province.
1871	The first legislature is organized.
1873	Winnipeg is incorporated as a city.
1874	A group of Mennonites, the first of several, arrive to take up land in southern Manitoba.
1875	A group of immigrants from Iceland set up the New Iceland colony on the west coast of Lake Winnipeg.
1876	The first shipment of Manitoba grain is sent to Toronto.
1877	The first railway locomotive arrives by steamship from St. Paul, Minnesota. The University of Manitoba is established.
1878	A railway is completed, connecting Winnipeg and St. Paul.
1881	The western boundary of the province is extended to its present location and the northern boundary to latitude 52°50'.
1884	The eastern boundary is established at its present location.
1885	The Canadian Pacific Railway completes its transcontinental line. Louis Riel is captured in the Northwest Rebellion, and is tried and executed at Regina.
1887	The Winnipeg Grain Exchange is established.
1890	The Manitoba School Act is passed withdrawing public support from Catholic schools and the Official Language Act makes English Manitoba's official language.
1892	The constitutionality of the Manitoba School Act is upheld by the Imperial Privy Council.
1912	Manitoba's northern boundary is set at the 60th parallel.
1916	Manitoba women become the first in Canada to win the right to vote in provincial elections.
1919	Winnipeg is paralysed for over a month by a general strike that ends in a violent clash between strikers and the police.
1927	The province's first pulp and paper mill is opened at Pine Falls.
1928	A copper-zinc mine is opened at Flin Flon.
1929	The Hudson Bay Railway to Churchill is completed.
1930	The natural resources of Manitoba are officially transferred to the province.

Information plaques along the Wall Through Time at the Forks mark significant events and periods in Manitoba's past.

1932 Drought and a world-wide depresssion cause the price of wheat to fall to a record low.

1940 Under the British Commonwealth Air Training Plan schools are set up at Brandon, Gimli, Portage, Rivers, Souris, Virden and Winnipeg to train air crew for the Second World War.

1950 The Red River overflows its banks, flooding much of the city of Winnipeg and surrounding farmlands.

1960 Nickel mining operations begin in Thompson.

1963 The first laboratories in the Whiteshell Nuclear Research Establishment go into operation.

1969 Manitoba voters elect Canada's second New Democratic Party government.

1976 The constitutionality of the 1890 Official Language Act is challenged.

1977 The Manitoba government agrees to compensate natives for damages caused by the flooding of the Nelson and Churchill Rivers by Manitoba Hydro.

1979 French is restored as a language of instruction in Manitoba public schools.

1980 The Supreme Court declares the Official Language Act of 1890 invalid.

1988 The Progressive Conservative Party returns to power, defeating the New Democrats.

1990 As a result of the actions of native MLA Elijah Harper, the Manitoba Legislature fails to ratify the Meech Lake Accord.

1992 The House of Commons unanimously passes a resolution acknowledging Louis Riel's contributions to Confederation.

1996 *Wapusk National Park*, Canada's seventh largest national park, is established southeast of Churchill.

William Barker

John Bracken

Douglas Campbell

Bobby Clarke

Important People

John D. Atchison (1870-1930), architect; designed nearly 100 buildings in Winnipeg between 1904 and 1922

William George "Billy" Barker (1894-1930), born in Dauphin; fighter pilot; credited with 53 First World War aerial victories; won the Victoria Cross when he fought alone against 60 German aircraft; first director of the Royal Canadian Air Force

Jackson Beardy (1944-1984), born at Island Lake; artist; noted for brightly coloured paintings that drew on his deep knowledge of Cree myths and legends

Margret Benedictssen (1866-1956), born in Iceland and immigrated to Manitoba; led Icelandic women's campaign to get the vote; founded Canada's first suffragist newspaper and Manitoba's first suffragist organization

Wilfred Bigelow (1913-), born in Brandon; heart surgeon; a pioneer in the use of hypothermia to protect the heart and brain from damage during long operations and in the development of pacemaker implants

Carol Bolt (1941-), playwright; born in Winnipeg; known for her ability to combine serious themes with humour and suspense; her best-known plays are *Buffalo Jump*, *Red Emma* and *Shelter*

John Bracken (1883-1969), politician; was Manitoba premier 1922-42; was head of the United Farmers of Manitoba; in 1942 agreed to lead the federal Conservatives if they added "Progressive" to the party name; resigned in 1948

Walter "Turk" Broda (1914-1972), born in Brandon; hockey player; goalie with the Toronto Maple Leafs 1937-52; won the Vezina Trophy in 1941 and 1948, and shared it in 1951

Lenny Breau (1941-1984), jazz guitarist; born in Maine but raised in Winnipeg by his parents, country singers Hal Lone Pine and Betty Cody; drew national attention in 1962, but his career blossomed in the U.S.

Sylvia Burka (1954-), born in Winnipeg; was a world class speed skater and cyclist despite the loss of one eye; won the world speed-skating championship in 1976 and 1977; set two world records; in cycling set world record for 1000 m in 1982

D.L. (Douglas Lloyd) Campbell (1895-1995), born at Portage la Prairie; politician, elected MLA in the riding of Lakeside in 1922; remained an MLA for 47 years, including 10 years (1948-1957) as Manitoba premier

Bruce Chown (1893-1986), medical researcher; pioneered

research into human blood groups and treatment of babies with Rh disease; was instrumental in setting up the world-renowned Rh laboratory for the study of blood groups

Bobby Clarke (1949-), born in Flin Flon; hockey player; overcame diabetes to play for the Philadelphia Flyers from 1969-84; had 358 goals and 852 assists

John Wesley Dafoe (1866-1944), journalist, editor of the Manitoba (later Winnipeg) *Free Press* from 1901-1944; one of the most influential journalists of his time

Lionel LeMoine FitzGerald (1890-1956), born in Winnipeg; painter; spent almost all of his life in Winnipeg painting and drawing quiet scenes; was principal of the Winnipeg School of Art 1929-47; joined the Group of Seven in 1930

Étienne Gaboury (1930-), born in Swan Lake; architect; designed many distinctive buildings in Winnipeg and elsewhere in Manitoba as well as in Mexico City and West Africa

Cuthbert Grant (c.1793-1864), fur trader, and a founder of the Métis nation; led the Métis group that fought with Selkirk settlers at Seven Oaks in 1816; later was appointed Warden of the Plains

Frederick Philip Grove (1879-1948), author; born in Hamburg, Germany; came to Manitoba in 1913; published essays, short stories and seven novels, the best known of which is *The Master of the Mill*

Dan Halldorson (1952-), born in Winnipeg; golfer; grew up in Shilo; turned professional in 1971 and joined the U.S. tour in 1979; won the 1980 Pensacola Open; strong supporter of Canadian golfing events

Evelyn Hart (1956-), ballerina; joined the Royal Winnipeg Ballet in 1976, became soloist in 1978, and principal dancer in 1979; in 1980, won the gold medal for best female soloist at the International Ballet Competition at Varna, Bulgaria

Barney Hartman (1916-), born at Swan River; judged by his peers the greatest skeet shooter in the world; claimed nearly 30 world titles

Doug Henning (1947-), born in Winnipeg; magician; became a star in 1974 with *The Magic Show* on Broadway; tours worldwide

Paul Hiebert (1892-1987), born at Pilot Mound; humorist, professor; taught chemistry at the University of Manitoba and was awarded the Governor General's Award for Science in 1924; best known for his satirical book *Sarah Binks* which won the Leacock Medal for humour in 1947

John Dafoe

Cuthbert Grant

Frederick Philip Grove

Evelyn Hart

Tomson Highway

Cora Hind

John Hirsch

Jerry James

Tomson Highway (1952-), born in Brochet; playwright; his two widely acclaimed plays, *The Rez Sisters* and *Dry Lips Oughta Move to Kapuskasing* combine high comedy with tragedy as they expose conditions on Canada's Indian reserves

Cora Hind (1861-1942), journalist, women's rights activist; became the West's first female journalist; agriculture editor of the *Free Press* from 1901; famous for accurately predicting the western Canadian wheat crop

John Hirsch (1930-1990), born in Siófok, Hungary; was one of the founders of the Manitoba Theatre Centre; went on to direct plays all over Canada and abroad; from 1981 to 85 was artistic director at Stratford

Jerry James (1935-), born in Winnipeg; football, hockey player; played football with the Winnipeg Blue Bombers and hockey with the Toronto Maple Leafs; scored 601 points with the Bombers, a team record

Stephen Juba (1914-1993), born in Winnipeg; politician; son of Ukrainian immigrants, he ran a successful business and served as an MLA before becoming Winnipeg's most colourful, controversial and popular mayor ever in 1956; re-elected eight times, once by acclamation; retired in 1977

Stanley Knowles (1908-), politician; represented Winnipeg North Centre for the NDP and its predecessor, the CCF, from 1942-58 and 1962-84; respected by all parties for his integrity and his knowledge of parliamentary procedure; when he retired for health reasons, Parliament made him an honorary officer of the House with a place for life at the Clerk's Table

Marie-Anne Gaboury Lagimodière (1780-1875), the first non-native woman known to have lived in the Canadian West; was Louis Riel's grandmother

Margaret Laurence (1926-1987), born at Neepawa; novelist; published her first novel in 1960; later published *The Stone Angel, A Jest of God* (Governor General's Award, 1966), *The Fire-Dwellers*, and *The Diviners*; also wrote four children's books

Dorothy Livesay (1909-), born in Winnipeg; poet, journalist, short story writer, feminist and literary critic; won the Governor General's Award for *Day and Night* (1944) and *Poems for People* (1947)

Nellie McClung (1873-1951), suffragist, author, legislator; raised in the Souris Valley; published the first of 15 books, *Sowing Seeds in Danny*, a national best-seller, in 1908; spearheaded the campaign for women's rights, in particular the right to vote, in Manitoba

Grace McInnis (1905-1991), born in Winnipeg; politician, daughter of J.S. Woodsworth; key member of the CCF and the NDP; influential backroom politician and respected MLA in B.C. (1941-45) and MP (1965-74)

Arthur Meighen (1874-1960), politician, Canada's ninth prime minister; set up a law practice at Portage la Prairie in 1896; was federal MP 1908-26; Conservative Party leader 1920-26, 1941-42; prime minister 1920-21, 1926; and senator 1932-41

Ovide William Mercredi (1946-), born at Grand Rapids; constitutional lawyer, aboriginal rights activist; practised law in The Pas 1979-82; elected Manitoba regional chief to the Assembly of First Nations in 1989 and National Chief in 1991

William Lewis (W.L.) Morton (1908-1980), born at Gladstone; professor; one of Canada's leading historians; won the Governor General's Award for *The Progressive Party in Canada* (1950); also wrote *Manitoba: A History* (1957) and *The Canadian Identity* (1961)

Bill Mosienko (1921-), born in Winnipeg; hockey player; played with the Chicago Black Hawks for 14 years; scored 258 goals and had 282 assists; on

March 23, 1952, scored three goals within 21 seconds against the New York Rangers

Andrew Mynarski (1916-1944), born in Winnipeg; war hero; was a Second World War gunner on a Lancaster bomber that caught fire; was awarded the Victoria Cross after he died trying to save a trapped comrade

John Norquay (1841-1889), born in the Red River Settlement; politician; elected to Manitoba's first legislature, was a cabinet minister through most of the 1870s; premier 1878-87

Sylvia Ostry (1927-), born in Winnipeg; economist, public servant; has held several senior economic positions in Canada and abroad; published works on demography, productivity and competition policy

Barbara Pentland (1912-), born in Winnipeg; composer; one of the first Canadian composers to use avant-garde techniques; composed for piano, orchestra, chamber ensemble and voice; her best-known composition is *Studies in Line* (1941), a set of four piano pieces

Thomas Prince (1915-1977), born at Petersfield; war hero; served in Italy and France during the Second World War and was Canada's most decorated soldier; elected chairman of the Manitoba Indian Association in

Dorothy Livesay

Nellie McClung

Arthur Meighen

Barbara Pentland

Thomas Prince

Gabrielle Roy

Edward Schreyer

Clifford Sifton

1946; served with the Princess Patricia Light Infantry during the Korean War

Louis Riel (1844-1885), Métis leader, acknowledged "father" of Manitoba; was leader of the Métis during the Red River Rebellion and largely responsible for Manitoba's entry into Confederation as a province; was arrested and executed at Regina for his role in the Northwest Rebellion of 1885.

Gabrielle Roy (1909-1983), born in St. Boniface; francophone author; won the Governor General's Award three times as well as many other literary awards; wrote movingly of her childhood and her years as a teacher in immigrant communities of rural Manitoba; also wrote stories for children

Terry Sawchuk (1929-1970), born in Winnipeg; hockey player; one of the greatest goalies of all time with a lifetime record of 2.52 goals-against average in 971 games; had a record 103 shutouts during his career

Edward Richard Schreyer (1935-), born at Beausejour; politician; Governor General of Canada, diplomat; premier of first NDP government outside of Saskatchewan in 1969-77; served as Governor General of Canada 1979-84, then as High Commissioner to Australia

Sir Clifford Sifton (1861-1929), politician, lawyer, businessman; moved to Manitoba from Ontario in 1875 and set up a law practice in Brandon; became Liberal MLA for Brandon and was elected to Parliament in 1896; responsible for the immigration policies that populated the Canadian west

Baldur Stefansson (1917-), born at Vestfold; plant scientist; worked with the plant science department of the University of Manitoba from 1952 until his retirement; internationally acclaimed for work that made it possible to grow rapeseed commercially

Vilhjalmur Stefansson (1879-1962), born at Arnes; explorer, ethnologist, lecturer, writer; one of Canada's most famous Arctic explorers; wrote many books and articles about the North; believed the Arctic was habitable and must be developed

Ken Watson (1904-1986), born in Minnedosa; curler; won 32 major curling events, including 6 Manitoba Bonspiel grand aggregate awards; developed innovations in technique, including the art of sliding while delivering rocks

Adele Wiseman (1928-1992), born in Winnipeg, author, educator; wrote short stories, plays and two novels, including *The Sacrifice*, for which she won the

Governor General's Award; wrote about Jewish life in Winnipeg's North End

George Woodcock (1912-1995), born in Winnipeg; author; wrote novels, poems, political analysis and literary criticism; won the Governor General's Award in 1966 for *The Crystal Spirit*, a book about George Orwell

J.S. (James Shaver) Woodsworth (1874-1942), born in Ontario; Methodist Minister, social worker, politician; was a federal MP from 1922-40; was a founder of the Canadian Commonwealth Federation (CCF), later to become the New Democratic Party

Adele Wiseman

Premiers of Manitoba

Alfred Boyd	None	1870-1871
Marc A. Girard	Conservative	1871-1872
Henry J.H. Clarke	None	1872-1874
Marc A. Girard	Conservative	1874
Robert A. Davis	None	1874-1878
John Norquay	Conservative	1878-1887
David H. Harrison	Conservative	1887-1888
Thomas Greenway	Liberal	1888-1900
Hugh J. Macdonald	Conservative	1900
Rodmond P. Roblin	Conservative	1900-1915
Tobias C. Norris	Liberal	1915-1922
John Bracken	UFM/Liberal Progressive	1922-1943
Stuart S. Garson	Liberal Progressive	1943-1948
Douglas L. Campbell	Liberal Progressive	1948-1958
Duff Roblin	Progressive Conservative	1958-1967
Walter Weir	Progressive Conservative	1967-1969
Edward R. Schreyer	New Democratic	1969-1977
Sterling R. Lyon	Progressive Conservative	1977-1981
Howard Pawley	New Democratic	1981-1988
Gary Filmon	Progressive Conservative	1988-

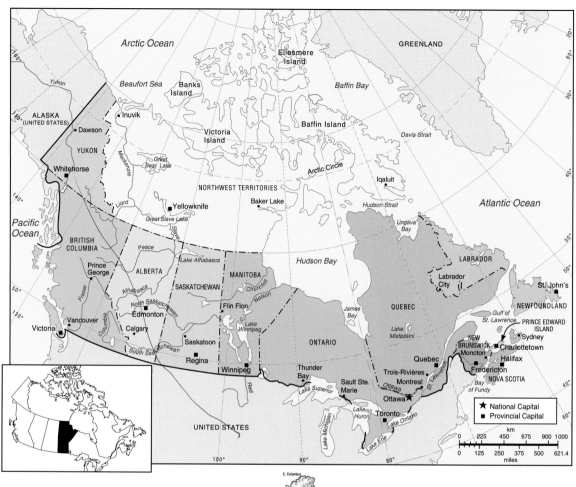

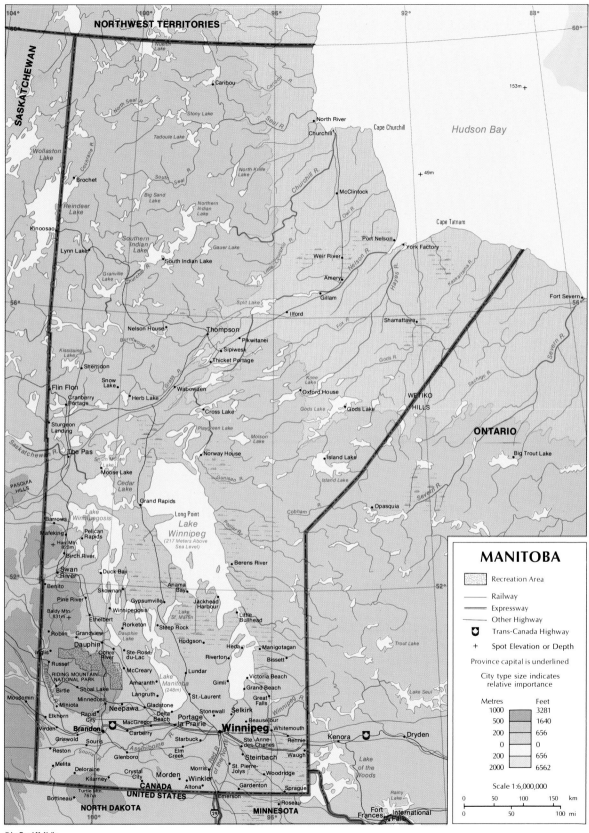

MANITOBA

Recreation Area

Railway

Expressway

Other Highway

Trans-Canada Highway

Spot Elevation or Depth

Province capital is underlined

City type size indicates
relative importance

Metres	Feet
1000	3281
500	1640
200	656
0	0
200	656
2000	6562

Scale 1:6,000,000

0   50   100   150 km

0   50   100 mi

© by Rand McNally

AVERAGE ANNUAL RAINFALL

The southeastern part of Manitoba receives the greatest amount of rainfall each year.

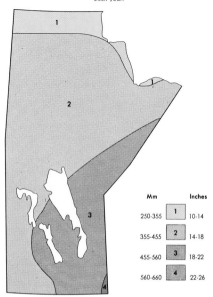

Mm		Inches
250-355	1	10-14
355-455	2	14-18
455-560	3	18-22
560-660	4	22-26

Figures within areas are for identification purposes only.

GROWING SEASON

Much of northern Manitoba has fewer than three frost-free months each year.

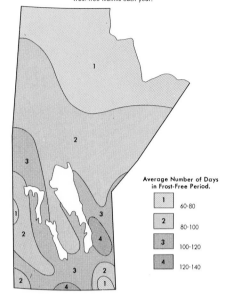

Average Number of Days in Frost-Free Period.

1	60-80
2	80-100
3	100-120
4	120-140

Figures within areas are for identification purposes only.

ECONOMY

HEAVY INDUSTRY
- Metal Processing
- St Steel
- Petroleum Refining
- Transportation Equipment

LIGHT INDUSTRY
- Chemicals
- Clothing
- Dairy Products
- Food Processing
- Lumber & Forest Products
- Metal Products
- Printing and Publishing
- Pulp & Paper Products
- Fishing

OTHERS
- Water Power

MINING
- Cu Copper
- G Gold
- N Nickel
- Pm Petroleum
- Ta Tantalum
- Z Zinc

AGRICULTURE
- Feed Grains & Livestock
- Wheat & Small Grains
- Fruit, Truck & General Farming
- Dairy Farming
- Grazing & Other Livestock
- Forests

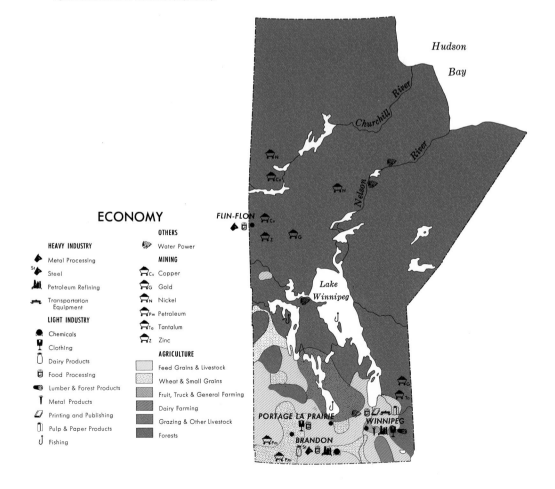

Hudson Bay

Churchill River

Nelson River

FLIN-FLON

Lake Winnipeg

PORTAGE LA PRAIRIE

WINNIPEG

BRANDON

Index

About the Author

Ken Emmond is a journalist, technical writer, and public relations and communications consultant who lives in Winnipeg. He graduated from the University of Manitoba with a B.A. and M.A., and from Carleton University with a degree in journalism. He has been a newsletter editor, and economic and political analyst as well as the author of eight books on world issues.

Picture Acknowledgements

Front cover, 23 (bottom), © Derek Trask/**The Stock Market Inc., Toronto**; 2-3, 4, 11 (top right), 16 (left), 17 (left and right), 19, 20 (middle left, centre, middle right and bottom left), 25 (top left and bottom), 34 (top right), 45 (top, left and right), 46, 56, 62 (right), 64, 65 (all), 66, 68, 71, 74 (all), 76 (bottom left and right), 84 (top), 88 (right, top and bottom), 89, 90 (background), 92 (left and right), 94 (right), 96 (bottom left and right), 98 (top), 100 (background), 104, 107, 111, © Brian Sytnyk/**Vis-U-Tel, Winnipeg**; 5, 6, 8-9, 11 (background and top left), 14 (left and right), 20 (top), 25 (top right), 45 (centre, bottom left and right), 68 (inset), 72, 76 (top), 77 (both), 78, 81 (right), 86, 88 (left), 90 (inset), 93 (left and right), 94 (left), 95 (left and right), 96 (top), 97, 113, © **Henry Kalen, Winnipeg**; 11 (top middle), 20 (bottom right), © Wayne Wegner/**First Light**; 16 (inset), 100 (flower), **Bill Ivy**; 18 (left/2642 and inset/10-1), 23 (top/148), 31 (right/Historic Sites Collection), 32, 34 (bottom/N3937), 36 (left/Red River Settlement 15 Collection), 39, 49 (top/N5776), 50 (bottom/N3081 and top right), 53 (School District #203 Collection), 55, 60, 61 (Transportation: Railway 19 Collection and inset/Draught 3 Collection), 62 (left), 116 (top/N9093/photo by London Chesney, middle top/W1719/Foote Collection, middle bottom/Campbell Collection, bottom/N9093/Manitoba Sports Hall of Fame Collection), 117 (top/Dafoe Collection, middle top/N12762/John Kerr Collection, middle bottom/Grove Collection), 118 (middle top/N978 and bottom/© Winnipeg Football Club), 120 (top), 121 (top/2117/Jewish Historical Society of Western Canada and bottom/Woodsworth collection), **Provincial Archives of Manitoba**; 20 (bottom right), 96 (bottom centre), 98 (bottom), © Dawn Goss/**First Light**; 23 (middle), **Les Soeurs Grises de Montréal, Maison Provinciale, Saint-Boniface**; 26-27 (912.1.24), **Royal Ontario Museum, Toronto**; 29 (top/C65104 and bottom/C5407), 31 (left/C1917), 36 (right), 38, 40, 42 (C19365), 43 (C6692), 50 (top/PA38567), 58 (right/PA30820), 119 (middle top/PA30212 and middle bottom/C691), 120 (middle top/C18347, middle bottom and bottom/PA33762), **Public Archives of Canada**; 29 (middle), **Metropolitan Toronto Reference Library**; 49 (bottom/NA-118-24), **Glenbow Archives**; 58 (left), **United Church of Canada Archives, Victoria University, Toronto**; 66 (inset), Derek Trask/**Superstock**; 81 (left), **Courtesy of Cercle Molière, Winnipeg**/Hubert Pantel; 82 (left), **Courtesy of the Royal Winnipeg Ballet**/Paul Martins; 82 (right), **BMG Music Canada**; 84 (inset), **Winnipeg Art Gallery**; 84 (bottom), © Paul Von Brick/**First Light**; 87 (left), **Courtesy of the Winnipeg Jets**; 87 (right), **Courtesy of the Winnipeg Blue Bombers**; 93 (centre), **Courtesy of the Museum of Man and Nature**; 99 (top and bottom), Mia & Klaus/**Superstock**; 100 (bird), Pat Morrow/**First Light**; 115, **Courtesy of the Forks Renewal Corporation, Winnipeg**; 117 (bottom), **Courtesy of the Royal Winnipeg Ballet**; 188 (top), **Michael Cooper**; 118 (middle bottom), **Courtesy of the Manitoba Theatre Centre**; 119 (top), **Department of Archives & Special Collections, The University of Manitoba**; 119 (bottom), © **Walter Curtin RCA**; back cover, © T. Klassen/**Hot Shots**.